William John Knox-Little

Characteristics and motives of the Christian life

ten sermons preached in Manchester Cathedral in Lent and Advent 1877

William John Knox-Little

Characteristics and motives of the Christian life
ten sermons preached in Manchester Cathedral in Lent and Advent 1877

ISBN/EAN: 9783741189845

Manufactured in Europe, USA, Canada, Australia, Japa

Cover: Foto ©Lupo / pixelio.de

Manufactured and distributed by brebook publishing software (www.brebook.com)

William John Knox-Little

Characteristics and motives of the Christian life

PREFACE.

OF the Sermons comprised in this volume seven [1] have been published in another form before. The remaining three [2] are now published for the first time. They were all preached *extempore*, and are corrected from reports made at the time. The mention of the places in which they were delivered, and allusions to the occasions of their delivery, as well as the forms of address to those who heard them, have been, for the most part, retained. It has been thought better that it should be so, as otherwise their character would have been entirely changed, and indeed it would have been necessary largely to rewrite them.

In revising the first six and the last, the author has retrenched the more obtrusive redundancies, corrected obvious mistakes, and (in places where the meaning was obscurely or inadequately conveyed) altered or added some words, expressions, and sentences.

[1] Sermons I., II., III., IV., V., VI., and X.
[2] Sermons VII., VIII., and IX.

PREFACE

They are published now (as those already in print were published at first) in accordance with the request of many who believe that they have found them helpful. They make no claim to be anything more than very slight discussions on some spiritual subjects.

The author trusts that they are, in all matters, in accordance with the teaching and spirit of the Catholic Church, as represented by the Church of England, and he hopes that they may be of some use to souls, in assisting them to live for God.

ST. ALBAN'S RECTORY, MANCHESTER,
Easter 1880.

CONTENTS.

I.
Christian Work.

"*I must work the works of Him that sent Me, while it is day: the night cometh, when no man can work.*"—ST. JOHN ix. 4 . . 1

II.
Christian Advance.

"*If ye then be risen with Christ, seek those things which are above, where Christ sitteth on the right hand of God.*"—COLOSSIANS iii. 1 26

III.
Christian Watching.

"*Watch therefore: for ye know not what hour your Lord doth come.*"—ST. MATTHEW xxiv. 42 47

IV.
Christian Battle.

"*Thou therefore endure hardness, as a good soldier of Jesus Christ.*"—2 TIMOTHY ii. 3 70

V.
Christian Suffering.

"*For it became Him, for Whom are all things, and by Whom are all things, in bringing many sons unto glory, to make the Captain of their salvation perfect through sufferings.*"—HEBREWS ii. 10. 96

VI.
Christian Joy.

"*Who for the joy that was set before Him endured the Cross, despising the shame, and is set down at the right hand of the throne of God.*"—HEBREWS xii. 2 118

VII.
For the Love of Man.

"*Bear ye one another's burdens, and so fulfil the law of Christ.*" —GALATIANS vi. 2 140

VIII.
For the Sake of Jesus.

"*Blessed are ye, when men shall revile you, and persecute you, and shall say all manner of evil against you falsely, for My sake.*"—ST. MATTHEW v. 11 162

IX.
For the Glory of God.

"*Whether therefore ye eat, or drink, or whatsoever ye do, do all to the glory of God.*"—1 CORINTHIANS x. 31 . . 197

X.
The Claims of Christ.

"*Come unto Me, all ye that labour and are heavy laden, and I will give you rest. Take My yoke upon you, and learn of Me; for I am meek and lowly in heart: and ye shall find rest unto your souls.*"—ST. MATTHEW xi. 28, 29 . 223

SERMON I.

Christian Work.

"I must work the works of Him that sent Me, while it is day: the night cometh, when no man can work."—ST. JOHN ix. 4.

I PROPOSE to speak to you, dear friends, upon certain aspects of the Christian life; not to go back into any of those fundamental questions about sin and conversion generally, or about special forms of sin, on which I had the opportunity of speaking to some in this Cathedral during the late Mission;[1] but to ask you to consider with me certain characteristic features of the Christian life—the life, I mean, not merely of a man who has heard of Christ, but of a man who has wakened up to His claim; who has wakened up to the effect and influence of the Lord's work, and has begun to realize the part which he himself must act, because that work has been done.

The text that I have read to you just now, comes from a story in which our Blessed Lord meant to teach us certain of the deep things of the laws of God. He

[1] A general mission was preached in Manchester in February 1877.

taught, by the particular work that He then was working, some of those mysterious principles of Divine government which, in their fulness, have been learned only from Him. He meant to correct certain erroneous statements and erroneous opinions about God's dealings with men, in physical suffering, or in mental weakness. He meant to stay some too hasty generalizations which had been made about the ways and the thoughts of God; but in the course of all that—and all that opens up to us a very wide field of thought and speculation—in the course of all that, our Blessed Lord, as it were, in passing, teaches us at least one very important truth about the Christian life. That is the point that I would insist upon for a few moments this afternoon. He teaches us that aspect of the Christian life which may be called its *aspect of labour*. He points out to us what it is we have to look for, if indeed we are Christians. He emphasizes the fact that for each one of us, if we mean really to face the full requirements of the Christian life, we must make up our minds to a life of labour.

To turn to God is one thing; to live to God is another. To turn to God, in very deed and very truth, with that hearty hatred of sin, and with that hearty love of Jesus, which are the very essence of a true repentance, to turn to God with that longing for pardon, which belongs to anything like a powerful faith, is one thing; to live for God, with the steady, persevering power of the Divine Spirit, is another, or rather it is an extension, farther on in the field of the soul's activity, of that great action which conversion has begun.

Well, let us ask ourselves this simple question: When we come to look at the Christian life as a life of labour, what is the value, what is the solemnity of the Christian's work?

And, first of all, I will meet the first point—What is its value? You will notice, then, if you look at our Master's saying, even though that saying is a kind of *obiter dictum*—even though it is "thrown in" (so to speak)—even though it appears to come out, almost in passing, in the midst of the story—you will notice, if you look carefully at our Master's saying, that the value of the work of a Christian consists, I may say consists altogether, in the *principle* which lies underneath or behind it. If, then, you would measure the value of your work as Christians, you have to look steadily at that principle. And as you come to think of the meaning and the dimensions of such a fact, you are reminded that *work*, as Christ looks at it, is not at all the expression of mere human activity. There are men, there are women—men and women of high capacities, of great mental endowments—who, in every division of human thought and human labour, have furrowed their track deep in the fields of history. There are men, as you all know, of scientific attainments, who have been powerful in illuminating the meaning of the laws of God with regard to the physical creation, before the minds of their fellow-men; men who have drawn out the secrets from this world, who have exposed to us the meaning of much that once we believed to be almost magical, and now is known to be only natural. There are men of historical power, who have been able to co-ordinate the various human motives and thoughts which have gone to form the springs of history, until they have succeeded, in part at least, in reading, some of those general laws of our great Creator, even in fields belonging not strictly to His divine revelation. There are, again, men of artistic faculties, who have been able—in throwing out thoughts upon canvas, which have startled us, sometimes with the beauty of execution, and always with the wonderful mystery of various colourings, combining into one picture before the eye—have been able, I say, thereby to exhibit to us, things that all mankind, more or less, have dreamed of, but that all mankind found themselves incapable to express. There have been men—as you and I, who live in this great city, know—who, by the mere activity of their life, have left a very deep impress upon their generation. But, after all, when we turn to the Christian life, we have to acknowledge, even without the divine revelation, that all that kind of work, all that outcome of what is mere human activity, is not at all *work* in the sense in which Christ means it, as becoming and glorifying an immortal. Not at all!

It is perfectly clear, of course, to all of us, that God's wisdom, "sweetly and wonderfully ordering all things," can, indeed, raise mere human activity into a powerful agent for executing His will. It is quite true, if you look over the history given to us in the Bible, or the histories that have come to us from human sources —it is quite true that men who can in no sense be said to have been working for God, have certainly done God's work. Judas was a kind of providential instrument in that which led to the redemption of the world. Pilate himself, in judging Christ, became also an instrument for that same divine end. The fiscal arrangements made by the Emperor Augustus, as he was regulating and governing the Roman empire, led, as we know, to the working out of that combination of circumstances, which had been pre-ordained for the birth of our Divine Redeemer. The insane cruelties, the insulting impertinences, that were characteristic of the apostate Emperor Julian, brought out the faith of Christendom more, and made men more to realize what God's work was for them. But would any men or women in their senses say that such people were working for God? Working they were—doing a great work, expressing themselves with astonishing activity—but, after all, however God turned this to His own glory, there remains the fact that it was not a work, in any sense, for God, and *that* because the principle which underlay it, was not that only principle capable of giving it such a character, according to the conditions set down by our Divine Redeemer.

Mere activity, then—and let us remember it when we have to take the value of our own life—is not that essential excellence in work—even when it witnesses to earnestness of character—is not that essential excellence that Christ would own. You may say, perhaps, "Surely it is, if you come to spiritual questions." I answer again, Certainly not. Mere activity, even if you come to a spiritual subject-matter, is not a work of God. To attend meetings which are meant to promote beneficial purposes, to go district visiting amongst the poor, to interest yourself in schemes for the advancement of mankind—nay, if I am to speak the truth, to preach sermons to men which may themselves move men's hearts nearer to God—these things are not necessarily works for God, and may possibly have in them no power of works for God at all, as regards the soul from which they emanate. Spiritual subject-matter does not create the work of the Christian, whether it be what we call his ordinary work of the world, or what we call, more distinctly, his religious efforts. Mere activity in a subject-matter itself good, is not the work of the Christian life. Again I answer, Certainly it is not!

If you are to estimate the value of that work, you must fall back upon the first thought I have reminded you of. Its real value—the real value that *you* will find in it at last, that *God* finds in it now—is altogether to be discovered by penetrating to the principle which lies underneath or behind it all. That is the first truth which our Blessed Master teaches us, in thinking of the Christian's life as a life of labour.

Well, before I pass on, pause for a moment, and think of this. You may say, "Then, after all, there are certain laws that our Redeemer Himself seems to have taught, which your principle *appears* at least to vitiate: 'The tree is known by its fruits,' says Jesus: if I am not to take the external working of a life, and try to go through it into that which lies underneath it, how am I to measure life at all?" Pardon me, that is precisely what you have to do. Do not rest *in* it, go *through* it. Certainly the exterior activity does not make *the* value of the work. Still it is not seldom the case, that the exterior activity takes its form and colour from the principle within, so that you are guided thereby in penetrating to that principle. But at all events you learn this; you learn to avail yourselves of Christ's teaching so far as to restrain yourselves from hasty criticisms: you learn, in fact, with regard to others, the law of charity; with regard to yourselves, you learn the stern, unflinching law of judgment. Not your mere activity in matters of the world, no, nor in spiritual things, goes to make up that work which is pre-eminently Christian. Again I answer, if any ask the question, Certainly not. The value of the work is to be measured by the principle which lies behind it.

Now, what is that principle? It is not difficult

to explain it, and I have no doubt whatever of your ready acceptance, for surely it is quite plain to us, if we think for an instant of what Christian work is, what must be the only principle that can give it any value at all.

Look behind the life of our Blessed Redeemer; doubtless you will see it there. Look behind His words; it is enunciated clearly enough in them. When you come to ask me, What is the principle? I answer, You will find it written in the Word in different ways; but plainly and shortly my meaning is this, *the will and the glory of God.*

Work, then—this Christian work—is not to be valued by its subject-matter; it is to be valued by that which lies behind it: *the* question is, whether or not it is done according to the will, and for the glory, of Almighty God. Look closely at the principle: Where will you see it readily? You will find it witnessed by two plain witnesses that no man can shut his eyes to, and the testimony of these witnesses is written everywhere.

(1) Through all, there is the corroborative testimony of *the reign of law* in physical nature. Go out into the outer world; stand at any time, in any clime, in any season; what is it you see? You find the spring-time coming, with all its glory, and life, and light, and loveliness; you find the summer advancing after it, bringing with it the beauties prepared by spring; you look on to the autumn, and the leaves are falling, and

the winds, as they whisper, tell you that winter is approaching, with its messages of death. Go out of the reach of the seasons and turn to the physical universe. Scientific men have thrown floods of light upon the marvellous history of that stately march which goes on, day by day, and night by night, when "the heavens declare the glory of God, and the firmament showeth His handiwork." They tell you that by the very seeming slowness, but real velocity, of these majestic motions, is measured the immensity of space, and that immensity itself, as it rises before our minds, surely witnesses to what is greater than immensity,—the infinity that lies beyond,—which is itself a shadow of God. But everywhere—in the animal creation, in the physical world about you, in the heavens you gaze upon at night, in the planet on which you live—one great truth, which comes out as a witness to offer its testimony, is this—*the reign of law;* and the reign of law throughout the universe says, "The will and the glory of God."

(2) There is another testimony, though, which comes nearer yourselves, which touches human life more closely than any witness drawn from the physical world; there is *the reign of moral freedom.* This concerns us all. We know perfectly well that a man, if he contradicts mathematical truth, is simply showing himself to be either an ignoramus or a fool. We know perfectly well that mathematical truth can be shown to be so absolute that it admits no sane contradiction. We acknowledge,

any one of us who has any education whatever, that the same is the case, in appropriate subjects, with the incisive witness of logic. Men dare not seriously contradict the one or the other, when they bring distinctly before them necessary truths.

Now there is another field of truth where fundamental facts of our being admit no contradiction from a sane, thinking man. There is the world of moral consciousness, that is, of consciousness of the power of an unfettered freedom of will, to choose the right or choose the wrong. Men may do which they please, but if they are true to that plain witness of the consciousness within them—the witness which I say is as clear and forcible as either logical truth or mathematical demonstration—if they are true to that, they have to acknowledge that God has bestowed upon them a wonderful power; and consequently that He has upon their life an indisputable claim. For God has by this gift inaugurated *the reign of moral freedom*—the freedom which is, above all, valuable because each mind, each soul, is thereby enabled to choose (that which, in the long run, is *the* one choice of life), to choose the object of its love. To have power to choose what you will to love, *that* is the greatest power, the most splendid endowment of a moral creature. And since *that* law of liberty is written in the heart of every man and woman in this Cathedral, God thus witnesses that you and I have each the power to choose the object of an everlasting love; to train, by reference to that object, all our life's emotions, to make *it* the ultimate aim of all our labours, all our toil. By the witness of that law which is written within us, by the fact that we may choose the right, there is a claim for the right to be chosen. By the fact that God has put that law within us, He advances His own imperious claim that we shall exercise it for the benefit of Himself Who gives it; and that power of moral choice, by which we are enabled to choose Him Who is the Highest as our object, witnesses, like the reign of law in creation, that the one end, the one object, the one aim of work, whatever the work may be,—of hand, or heart, or head,—if it is to be valuable in a Christian sense, must be this—*the will and the glory of God.* My brothers, I challenge you to contest that witness.

But if for a moment you doubt that testimony, let me call two more witnesses into court. Or rather, let me go on for a moment with this last sort of evidence, giving it precision by one mouthpiece. If you doubt that the aim of your work really gives value to it, and that therefore, if it be Christian work, that aim must be the glory of God, question your *conscience.* If you have learned to love the Lord Jesus Christ, in any measure; if you have learned to turn to Him with anything like a deep devotion; if Jesus has come before you as a Sovereign to rule, a Friend to guide you, He does so, amongst other ways, by quickening *that* power within you by the voice of the Spirit. Question your conscience. You may pardon a man many things, but for disobeying that witness you will scarcely pardon him. You may pardon a man for being foolish, for being faulty; you may forgive him because he is wanting in culture, or because he does not exercise his endowments as well as he might, in the ordinary walks of life; but, as a thinking creature going through life, you will scarcely pardon him if you find he is habitually not a conscientious man. You will demand—if he is a Christian, or (if he does not call himself that) if he is a moral being—you will demand that he shall act conscientiously. Question your own conscience, then, out in active life, or in the inner life of religion—reading your Bibles, or working in the world—what does that "still small voice" within you whisper from time to time? If you have turned to God, and given Him anything of your love, how are you pouring it out upon Him? Is your work done *for Him?* Why are you doing it? How are you doing it? Are you doing it with any admixture? With anything as ultimate end, but Him alone? Alas! probably you are, but if so, in the still moments of the soul there is some uneasiness. Does not that witness come before you again and say, The *principle* which makes work, Christian, is, *the will and the glory of God?*

Or (and I think this Witness will win for you even greater attention: I hope so: I hope that the Name of this Witness will call out your hearts more than the name of conscience) there is another Witness, and He speaks from the text. It is Jesus, our Master: ask Him how He bore testimony, how He bears it this afternoon; how, in the midst of our working life, how, in the midst of our religious thought, how, in our times of devotion, how, in our hours of prayer, He still speaks to us, and bears that unflinching testimony, calling upon the Christian to persevere making his work true.

He does it, I submit to you, in three ways. (1) He does it because He has robed Himself in our humanity. Robing Himself in our humanity, Jesus has added a dignity to our nature. It was made in the image of the eternal: it was created indeed with *that* stamp upon it, which even original sin could not altogether wipe out. But Jesus, by the Incarnation, has done something more. He has robed Himself—Most High God—in that nature: thereby He has added dignity; and by the fact that you have been dignified, by your nature being taken "into God," by that fact you are taught that the dignity of that nature is never satisfied, unless entirely you aim in your work to do God's will, and set forth God's glory. So He has borne, and is bearing, His witness.

(2) He bore it, let me remind you further, by Himself toiling and teaching in that nature; He showed to you and me not only its dignity—He showed its power. The power of human nature is all but infinite—all but infinite as seen in the work it can do, when it is

assisted by the power which our Blessed Master exerted on it—by the power of God. Teaching us what the power of human nature may be when joined to the Eternal, our Lord witnessed again to the principle which enhances, which gives the value to, all our work. You have—in a sense—power to do even as God does, rising up into the life of God; God *is* perfection, you have power to *aim at* perfection; God must, then, be the object of all.

(3) Need I add that He witnessed it by His death? Not only by being robed in humanity, not only by showing the power of humanity for God, but by dying in this humanity; by exhibiting to us, in this way, the immensity of the value that God placed upon it, He taught us its only end in labour. Go to His work in life, hang on His teaching lips, gaze at His lacerated form on the Cross—however you look at Him, and wherever, the witness of Jesus is ever the same. It is this: "Believing child, My child, you have loved Me, you have sought your pardon from Me, you have asked Me to help you to bear the burden, to wash away the sin, to illuminate the conscience, to quicken the heart. Oh, if I am to warm your affections, if I must strengthen your will, what are you to do in return? Work your work while it is called to-day—the work which is valuable, according to My witness, in proportion as the principle that guides, and rules, and stimulates, is the same as that to which I have witnessed in every part of

My life—the same that was taught in the agonies of My dying—*the will and the glory of God.*"

If the Christian is to do his work, it does not matter about the dimensions of its outward expression; it does not matter about the texture of the material; the great point for you and me to see to, is that *the principle* lying behind it be real, one that is maintained in its reality by the grace of the Blessed Spirit, by the example of our Divine Redeemer—that principle being—that its aim and object are—*the will and the glory of God.*

Dear friends, such, I venture to say, is the true value of Christian work. And now, for a moment, I have to remind you that you have a method of measurement to test the value of your own. Apply it to your life's work. Are you working for God? I don't say, "Have you returned to God?" I asked that question often enough when I had opportunities lately of speaking to souls in this Cathedral; but this afternoon I would ask the further question, "Turned to Jesus, are you *working* for God?" The Christian life is not a life of sloth; not a life of dreaminess. The value of the work of that life lies in this great principle, renewed and exerted from time to time, not the mere saving of one's own soul, though that was the first point—but, getting beyond that, expressing continually in the world the principle which is the heart of that soul's salvation—the love of God's will, the desire for God's glory.

Are you doing it? Are you trying to do it? Is there

any one here this afternoon to whom I was enabled to speak in the late Mission? If there be; if *you* listened to any word that came from God through me; if *you* listened to any voice of that Spirit that spoke in your soul, what is the result? Have you set about more earnestly the work of a Christian? Have you set about to measure all you do—not your religious action only, though that pre-eminently, but *all* your action, wherever it be—in the outer world, in the quiet home, in the Church of God—by that one true test of its being the work that He has called you to do—by its real principle of valuation, how far it is conformed to the will, how far it aims at the glory of God.

You may say, perhaps, "Yes, but how am I to read that will? I do love God; I have turned to Jesus; I know Him for my Redeemer; I have longed for His love; I have brought my sins to Him; I have been in real earnest. Nay, more, I have known the joy and benediction of what it is to love Him, in some measure, even though it may be in small; but how am I to know the truth of my work by this text, how am I to know what *is* the will of God?"

There are two things at least that will guide you—the one, your special capabilities; the other, the circumstances of your life. You have different capacities. We have all of us special endowments; each has got some place in the providential ordering of God; not one soul but has his or her place. God has given each a work. His will for you is to be measured by the capabilities that you have. Some have power of brain, some of heart, some of hand. Some can illuminate a quiet home, by the tender brightness of a holy life; some can lead vast masses of their fellow-creatures by a splendid example of energetic and determined fixity of purpose; some can think of God with peculiar depth and power in quiet times, when alone with Him. They can so meditate that the meditation of their soul is felt, rather than heard, by those who associate with them in life. Some can go forth into the great working world, and speak, or do a work, for God amongst those around them. But for each one, old or young—O loved of God, O child of Jesus, O turned to the Master with a whole heart and a loving determination—for each, therefore for *you*, there is a special work in the history of this universe. See what the capacity is He has given you, what the circumstances are in which He has placed you, and then go and do your work by the power of the love of Jesus that is given to you, by the strength of the Spirit which is poured out upon you, with the aim, the everlasting, the unchanging aim, which gives all value to the weakest toil—the fulfilment of the will, and the glory of God revealed in Jesus Christ our Lord.

Such is the value of the Christian's work. And now a word as to its solemnity. It is not only valuable; it is solemn. Mark me, I speak accurately when I say solemnity; I do not say gloom. In the oldest heathen nations there was a gloom that wrapped around all human life, because there was such a mysterious, dim anticipation of an unknown somewhat, that they could not measure, could not explain. All their poetry, all their prose, their great thoughts, their lesser fancies, are dashed across with that stain of gloom. But once Christ is come, human life indeed has still about it a robe of mourning, but that robe is not one of gloom, but of solemnity. Work your work while it is called to-day! That indeed is the duty; and the principle is, "for the glory of God." What is the solemnity? The night is coming: "the night cometh when no man can work." Yes, the night is coming, it is hastening on. It may be early morning with you, but at least you are advancing towards noon. It may be the glory of the noonday, but, indeed, while the shadows do not fall around you, they are gaining imperceptibly, at last to fall. It may be the quiet afternoon, but recollect the gloaming is advancing, and the evening will come. The evening! It is marked in different ways, supplying sober solemnizing thoughts; and hence it gives to the work of advancing years—solemnity. You will find within your breast the waning power of the exercise of influence you had in your home; you find the difficulty, more than ever, of fighting down some wretched habit for which not only do you want forgiveness, but which, too, you desire to conquer for the love of Jesus; you find, perhaps, the witness of a failing memory, or of failing health; you find that in some way or other the finger of God is touching you. The world may not see it; friends may not read it; those who are dear to you may not tell it; but *you* know it—the witness, whatever it is, is come—is coming. It speaks to you in the silence of the night. It wakens with you when you waken in the morning; it travels with you as a settled consciousness, when you are going about the world; it is the whisper of that unrelenting law of unchanging changefulness—"the night is coming." Oh, the Christian's work—the work of one who has loved Jesus—is solemn, for the results are infinite, and the time is short; you will not then pause on the journey, you will not stay on the threshold, you will not be content merely to turn to Him—content, with His having forgiven you, my brother, my sister? Ah, no! "The night is coming, when none can work."

Work then with that aim and that object; work with that strength and that endeavour which He gives you, work because of the advancing of time; because you and I,—each with the work that none other can do but ourselves,—you and I are getting on towards the night which is coming, when no man can work. That is the solemnity of the Christian's work. Other men hardly waken up to it. They know that death is coming: they know that trite fact, and they forget it; but the Christian wakens up to the thought of death, with the solemn recollection that he has a special work to do according to God's will and for God's glory, and that unless *he* does it, it will not be done. He knows that his Master has called him to one special place in His kingdom; he is not going to turn aside from *his* place because other men have theirs.

Each of you, if you be Christians indeed, feeling that the end is coming, will struggle the more to get the work well done before it comes. Jesus did it! Should not you and I? Jesus set the example: should we not follow? Oh! up and on, in all your activities; but recollect keep the principle right, at the bottom of it all. Recollect, by practising prayer, recollect, by seeking grace, recollect, by going back on the tracks of your actions (to examine and see whither they have been leading you), recollect—measure the value of your work, not merely by its activity but by the true aim which is set before you all.

One word to conclude. If that be the value of Christian work, if that be its solemnity; well then what is it we can take to ourselves to emphasize such facts in our own souls? Surely this; remember, first, we live in an age of intense activity; remember the truth of the assertion that "the factory and the steam-engine are only images and symbols of the times" to which you and I are born; that we live in a world which no longer only *examines* the agencies of nature, but *seizes* those agencies, and applies them to its own domestic purposes; remember that in the midst of this vast activity there is a solemn teaching, a severe temptation—a teaching of the magnificence of labour, a teaching of the glory of toil, a teaching of the necessity of earnest devotion to an object. A temptation, also, besides the teaching—the temptation to forget, in outer activity, that we have to look up, above, and through it all, to Him "Who giveth all;" —the temptation to forget that God is the Object of all true life. Be warned of the temptation and make your work well founded by the lofty aim of your Christian life. There is that to remember: this also—that all our work, whatever it be, is such, that we have no means indeed of accurately measuring—that we need not care accurately to measure—its entire power and its entire consequence. I maintain that not one human creature in this Cathedral this afternoon, can measure accurately the full power or consequence of his or her work for God. You cannot tell it here: you can only see that it is really valuable in so far as you are keeping to the principle of doing His will. You can only know that it *will* bring consequences which must at last be glorious, if you take care to fall back upon that root-principle. Your power you cannot tell, though every day you have been exercising it, and the consequences that follow from the exercise of that power, O soul,—loving Jesus, living in His strength—those consequences—all that you and I can say about them, thank God, is just this —that they are eternal, and that their eternity will be one of glory, in that they result from a work, of which the root-principle is submission, devotion to the will and glory of God. Morning by morning, evening by evening, and mid-day by mid-day, let us go back into the quiet secret converse of the soul with God: "My God, am I doing this for Thee? My God, help me to do this for Thy glory. Fill me with a longing for the working out of Thy will."

Then, be sure of it, let the subject-matter of your work take care of itself; do it as "the hand may find it to do," be it in the quiet life of home, or hard work in the factory, or brain-work in the study, be it the ordinary work of the Christian in society, never mind about the subject-matter: "Whatsoever thy hand findeth to do, do it with thy might," and since you are again and again trying to learn, drink in, and apply the true principle, then the power of your work is infinite, and its consequences will be eternal.

O mother in this congregation, with your children to train; O father that lookest forth on thy boys with anxiety, and art desirous to lead them right; O young man or young woman, thrown out into the world to work or toil, oh *do* learn how the great apostle has showed you to measure your work. Thrown into all sorts of circumstances, placed in all kinds of trial, he had learned one lesson—that he must work "to-day"—that if he did little, it mattered not what the subject-matter was, so that the principle was right; and therefore it was that he was able to say—what you and I must learn to say increasingly—"I have learned, in whatsoever state I am, therewith to be content."

Are you broken in health? Are you shattered in constitution? Are you weary of your toil? Are you day by day finding life hang heavy? My brother, my sister, you still have a work to do, if you love Jesus; for, *whatever* comes to you each day, is done with that aim; *whatever* comes to you each day, is referred to that object; and so—recollect my words and mark the witness of Christ and His apostles to their truthfulness—the power of your work will be infinite, and the consequences eternal in glory. Oh, what a stimulus to activity (to the real activity of the soul and of the brain) if we seriously think of these things!

And last of all we have to beware lest, when we are working at God's work in the world, we shall from time to time forget the aim. We have to watch ourselves most closely. Conversion is the beginning, not the end, of life. After conversion, work and battle. After that, coming back to Jesus; then toil for Jesus.

Take care and watch to be not proud if He has received you; to be not self-confident if He has forgiven you; but in humility, and earnestness, and determination, see to it, that henceforth it shall not be self but Jesus: that you will go on steadily, and yet try never to be puffed up, lest indeed you should fall. The seriousness of your work you best can realize, as your Master realized the seriousness of His. In Him it gathered solemnity from one governing thought, and so it must in you. Live and work in the recollection of death.

Live, not with its gloom, but with its solemnity; think of it as the entrance to the unimagined wonders of the region of rest and splendour, where He will take the measure accurately, and gather up the consequences.

O lost lives, wasted lives, that begin in nothing, go on in nothing, end in nothing, how awful it all is to them! But to you—with that aim before you, that power within you—it is serious, but surely also blessed! Have your moments of trial, your moments of temptation, your thoughts of worldliness, been brightened, or governed, or restrained, by the recollection of that final coming, when the bounding horizon shall recede to infinite distances before you, and the measure of all that is done shall be taken—taken for eternity? Is it so? Well, what then? He will come—for He is intensely merciful—He will come, as the Psalmist tells us, and what will He do? Do you dream a *reward* for your working? How can you hope it? Have you and I not darkened and vitiated all we have touched, by something unworthy of that Divine Ideal. But He will come, none the less, so the Psalmist says, to us, to the Christian who lives for Him, and "He will reward"—think!— "*reward* every man according" as his work shall be.

Oh, wonderful condescension! oh, marvellous mercy! Look forward to that joy. Be up and be active. Go back to the toil of the Christian; be not slack; be not ashamed; be not slothful; be not afraid. Storm the fort of the enemy; stand against the fierce temptation;

witness to the "Truth as it is in Jesus;" live in the world as those who are for eternity; and then He will come, when all is over, when the work is done, and the night is gathering around you—in the shrouds of its darkness, the intensity of its gloom, the anguish of its fear;— He will come to you with the witness and the sign of His Passion. He will give you Himself—crown of all gifts He can give you—your joy, your support, your comfort, and (remember, O Christian, who have worked for Him) your " exceeding great *reward.*"

SERMON II.

Christian Advance.

"If ye then be risen with Christ, seek those things which are above, where Christ sitteth on the right hand of God."—COLOSSIANS iii. 1.

IT is in these heart-stirring words, dear brothers, that the Apostle Paul tries to enforce upon those who had been converted to Christ at Colosse, the duty of higher, braver efforts in the Christian life. I tried to remind you on a former occasion, that the Christian life, after it had become a fact, and a reality—after, that is to say, the soul had given itself to God with an earnest intention—was a life that implied, as well as glorified, labour; and that it must imply and glorify it to the end; and to-day, I would try to put before you, what the Apostle Paul is insisting upon in the text—that *that* life of the Christian, is, in relation to God, indeed, no stagnant life, nor yet life of mere toil; but that the toil, if it be true, must be leading a man higher and higher; that, in fact, it is an *advancing life.*

Notice, for a moment, the connection of St. Paul's words with his previous thought. St. Paul, in this beginning of the Epistle to the Colossians, has been setting forth in a masterly way the special work of our Redeemer. He has been insisting to the Colossians that (instead of submitting to the heresy which had been attracting their attention and enchaining their thought, instead of accepting, as that heresy would teach them, a strange and fantastic string of mediators) they must recognise that there was One great Mediator, Who by His office, whether in the old creation or in the new, was the sole power, spiritual and effective, that could unite this lower world with its Creator.

St. Paul had passed on from that doctrinal statement of the mediatorial office of Christ, which we find in the first chapter and the early part of the second chapter of this Epistle; he had passed on to find fault with the entire ethical system, as well as the special precepts, which belonged to the heresy. With merciless logic he had attacked all their strongholds; he had been pitiless towards them, in trying to drive out those materialistic conceptions, which made this heresy at Colosse the great forerunner of the later Manichean impieties that devastated the Church; he had been merciless also in overthrowing the idea that had sprung up amongst them, of the necessity of galvanizing into a sort of new and fictitious life the old forms of Judaism. Nor had he done only so much; but with equally destructive criticism, he had made short work of the philosophical element in their heresy. He had taught these Colossian

Christians that the "Wisdom" that men had brought to take the place of the Gospel of Christ, though indeed it was put forward in forms of philosophy, was, after all, utter madness, whether on its philosophical, on its materialistic, or on its Jewish side. The heresy pervading their Church, St. Paul said, was first and last false and misleading, and in place of it he goes on in the text,—after he has attacked that heresy in all its departments (for in all those three departments he does attack it, as you see, if you observe carefully what he says in the previous chapter),—after so attacking it, he goes on in the text to put before them the energetic, earnest, fruitful, faithful life that springs from the Gospel of Christ.

And first, I would have you notice the *basis* upon which St. Paul puts forward his view of the life of the Christian, as a *life of advance*. The basis is this: he maintains, and maintains earnestly, to those to whom he wrote, that their life had passed through a crisis. He warns them that there had been a special time, marked by a special external witness, when that life had advanced out of one sphere of being into another, when they had stepped off one platform of thought on to another; and therefore, because upon the fact of this momentous change he based his view of their life, the exhortation of the text had real force.

Notice, before I go on, how essential it is to recognise that basis. Christianity is not a mere matter of feeling and emotion. Christianity has indeed in its keeping forces capable of drawing forth the warmest emotions, and kindling the most glowing feelings of the human heart. But Christianity in its very essence is something deeper than that; and as the Christian life, on its *subjective* side—on the side of the soul—is something more than feeling, so that on which it rests *objectively* is something more than mere idea. The *basis* of it all is fundamental fact. St. Paul is insisting upon this. He turns to his converts and says, "I have swept away your 'Wisdom;' I have crushed your materialism; I have denied your old Judaic thoughts. Why? Because these fancies are needless as well as false; because there is a fact at the basis of your spiritual life; because you have passed through a crisis; you *died* with Christ—and, more, you rose again with Christ. Not that you are dying, not that you are rising; but you *did die*—actually *die*—in a real though a mystical sense; you *did rise*—actually *rise*—in a sense equally real though equally mystical." The fact, then, is that the regenerating grace of the Spirit of God, acting upon the soul of the creature that God has formed, has the power to place—ay, and places—that soul, in a state of death, as regards the mere world around it, in a state of resurrection as regards that higher world above. Now, on that fundamental fact—a fact which St. Paul speaks of as being indisputable—he bases the exhortation of the text, teaching that the Christian life is henceforth a *life of advance*.

Well, then, before I go further, let me remind you that what St. Paul would have you all to recognise is—that where God's grace has touched the soul; where that regenerating grace, once given, has, further, been fully realized and surrendered to; where converting grace, reviving the flagging spiritual energies, has been brought home and acted upon—has been appropriated, has been coalesced with, by the powers of the soul,—that henceforth, where that is the case, the real power of the Christian life is a deepening, increasing, steadying conviction of the wholly changed sphere of its action, of the wholly altered platform where it stands. Realize that fact first. Recollect that, if you have turned to God, have listened to His call; recollect that, if you have taken Him at His word and submitted to Jesus, the platform of your life is changed, the sphere of your activity is altered, and that then you start not merely to a life of labour, but to something higher, better, grander than labour—an *advance* upward and onward on a new and glorious course.

It is not unnecessary to insist upon this. There are minds which are apt—only too apt—to look upon the Christian life as a life of mere stagnation. There are minds apt to look on the converting grace of God, as being a power that, having made its presence felt in souls, henceforth acquits them of any further effort to go on towards glory. There are some who are satisfied with having been awakened, satisfied with having realized a part of the truth, satisfied with having grasped the great thought of conversion, and the greater thought of the forgiving love of Jesus our Redeemer. I entreat, my brothers, that you and I shall not be among these, that you and I shall not thus be satisfied—I insist that, on the contrary, we must remember that there remains before us *the advancing life*. Because you *rose again* with Christ—for that is the force of the apostle's thought—therefore "seek the things that are above, where He sitteth on the right hand of God."

Well, then, let me remind you next of this: That Christianity, in urging us to that advance, is falling in with the fundamental fact and experience of our nature. It does not need regenerating grace, it does not need a converting call, to tell us men that there is within us a yearning and a longing for higher things. "Oh that I had wings like a dove!" says the Psalmist, "for then would I fly away, and be at rest." "We have an idea of happiness," says a great French writer, who has bequeathed, as a legacy, the stray but profound imaginings of his mind about God—"we have an idea of happiness, and yet we cannot grasp it; we are conscious of an image of the True, yet we possess only the False. There is an ignorance; yet not absolute. There is a knowledge; yet not certainty." Yes. We are always haunted by a memory or stimulated by a hope. We are always looking after something; we hardly know what it is. All seems unreal: no, not all! David felt it, Pascal felt it. You and I have felt it. There are moments in life when the soul will yearn and long for something beyond; moments when nature herself seems to feel it; times when the most thoughtless waken up to an aspiration which nothing in this world can satisfy. That fundamental fact of our consciousness, like all other fundamental facts, is more than met, is steadied, by the Gospel of Christ. Ye are "risen with Christ," and *therefore* do not merely have yearnings, do not merely have indefinite longings, do not merely look to "a beyond," to which you can hardly give any sort of definite meaning, but "seek *those things* that are above, where Christ sitteth on the right hand of God."

Well, then, my brothers, what is it that Christianity does for us, in teaching us that *to advance* is a characteristic of the Christian life? It possesses itself of our natural yearnings, of those mysterious longings which we have by right of the dignity and sorrow of our moral nature—these it takes, and before them it places objects sufficiently powerful and attractive, to give them precision. It gives precision to what was vague before. You and I have henceforth the definite "somewhat;" we are no longer grasping after shadows and clouds.

Now what is that definite "somewhat"? What is it the apostle offers to us as the guiding star of our advance? My brothers, I answer at once, "The things that are above." But here you object, "Well, again you are indefinite." Yes, I grant you in a certain sense. I grant you that, in a certain sense, I cannot speak more precisely. Who is to measure, who to catalogue, "the things which are above"? And yet what Christianity DOES say to you is, they *are real facts.* Christianity makes your yearnings precise, because it tells you to strive after that which is at once real and attainable. We talk of spiritual gifts; we talk, in our higher moments, of divine illuminations; we talk of whispers from another world. Spiritual gifts, divine illuminations, the whispers of the Spirit of God *are eternal treasures.* What St. Paul would remind you of, is the fact, that it is not a vague, a shadowy thing that you are groping after, but a real treasure from a real treasure-house. Call them what you may; leave them unnamed if you cannot name them; call them by the name he gives them if you find no better—glorious murmurs of God striking your ear with sounds of eternity—whispers of the Spirit, that tell you tales which are "mystic, wonderful,"—"the secrets of the Lord" to "them that fear Him;" spiritual gifts and graces within you—these are "the things which are above."

Can we, then, know nothing of them more precise than this, if by their attraction we are to hope for advance in spiritual life? I think we can. This at least: we can learn something of their power and beauty by observing their effects on character.

First, then, those who do "seek the things which are above," as a matter of fact become elevated in *tone and temper.* Do not think that tone and temper are nothing. In the best pictures of great masters, *tone* is almost everything. Form goes for much. Form, indeed, and the steadiness of the drawing, go for very much in the "composition" of the picture; but deprive it of the wonderful *non so che* called *tone*, and it stands out hard and unpleasing, and supplies to the soul no real pleasure. On the other hand, let the *tone* of the true artist be there, and how it covers in a great degree even badness in the drawing. In the same way, in nature, atmosphere counts for much, very much, in the charm of a scene, in its power, that is, to touch the heart; and when you come to personal life, what *tone* is to the picture, what *atmosphere* is to the landscape, such is general temper to the human character. Now the power and beauty of "the things which are above"—and the consequent necessity and blessedness of seeking them—all this is placed in evidence by the altered temper of the life in an *advancing* Christian. There are men with whom you meet, with just the same sort of gifts, with much the same kind of natural character, and yet how different! In some you are struck with the earnestness and effort displayed in a consistent pursuit of the things of this world; in others with a mysterious "something" not easily defined, and which yet touches you whenever you meet them. You find about them an extraordinary simplicity, a striking earnestness, a strange quietude. As a Christian, you call it an "interior spirit." It is not that they neglect common duties. No, they do them more precisely than before. It is not that they forget human interests. No, they can fling themselves into the noblest enterprises of their age. It is not that they are chilled in natural sympathies. No, their affections are wide and deep, and without words, you *feel* how large-hearted they are. It is, that in all these things there has come down upon them an influence from God. Feeling it, and face to face with an eminent instance, you say to yourselves, "The tone and the temper of the life of the man is altogether different from anything we have met before." My brothers, have you not experienced something of this *sort* at least, if not in the highest *degree*, in your active life? Have you not found something like it in some fellow-workman with whom you walk the steps of life—your companion in ordinary labour? If so, have you not noticed how he can talk of common things, read his daily paper, do his office-work, take an interest in the amusements, even, which in your young life you select to cheer you? And yet about him there is that "somewhat," that *tone and temper* which changes all—"simplicity," "earnestness" you call it—"quietude," or "interior spirit"—well, you cannot find the word; never mind: you see at least that it is a *something* from another world.

Shall I tell you the secret? Shall I explain the mystery? That soul, wherever he is, has been "seeking those things which are above." He has recognised the fact that his sphere of being is an eternal sphere, and in that sphere he is acting, on whatsoever stage of this life he has to play his part.

There[1] are not wanting in history, as there are not wanting in the life of to-day, instances of men possessed of excellent natural gifts, considerable influence, and even no inconsiderable power of attracting others, the evening of whose days is darkened by an increasing sense of the emptiness and insipidity of life, while yet, so weak has their faith been, or their search for "things which are above" so feeble, that while "old things are passing away" from them, in their place comes nothing new. How different is the case with those whose faith is strong, whose search for "things which are above" has been earnest and persevering! It is recorded of a Frenchman of some eminence in the clerical world of the sixteenth century [2]—a man of extraordinary self-denial, of extraordinary sweetness of character and sanctity of life—recorded by an eloquent orator who pronounced his panegyric long years after his death, that the only thing that ever seemed to make him

---

[1] The following passage I have rewritten in some measure. In the former edition it stood in the form of a contrast between two men, whose lives seemed to me illustrations of the worldly and spiritual mind. I have since had reason to believe that I had misinterpreted the cause of sadness in one of them, and that he was not insensible to the things above; I have therefore altered the passage; of the cause of serenity in the other's life I have no doubt, and so I have kept the reference to him.

[2] Fourier.

really miserable, was when he came face to face with any one who appeared unconscious of the blessedness of the love of God. At other times, his life, though severe and laborious, was sunny, bright, quiet; always serene, simple, steadfast; always attractive, not only from gifts with which God had gifted his nature, but by "a somewhat," which could not, according to ordinary methods, be explained. We can explain it. The apostle tells us the difference between such a man and one possibly more skilled in the world's ways, but a stranger to that sweet serenity. The worldling, or the man of feeble faith, whatever be his natural gifts, lives habitually in a sphere of sense, or intellect; God's servant exercises a loftier capacity, he realizes a sphere of life immeasurably more blessed, he is "seeking those things which are above."

"Seek those things which are above," and the *tone of life* is changed.

Is there any further effect of "heavenly things"? It is not only true that the tone of life is changed by "seeking" them, but also that the *sphere of thought* is enlarged. I must not dwell upon this, but only say, Recollect, O Christian, that it is false to think that only scientific truth, only historical fact, only the news of the politics of the day, only mathematical demonstration can really enlarge thought. Recollect that moral truth, when dwelt upon, enlarges thought more than all else.

More than all else? No. Spiritual truth, "the things which are above," even more.

The thought of God enlarges thought. To realize more His Providence, to see His Fatherly care applied to life, not only eases the shoulder of the burden of daily anxieties, it does more: it enlarges our view of the meaning of the past history of humanity. It enlarges our view of men around us in daily life. Why do we hesitate to give cut and dried answers about individual character or individual situations? Because we have been learning to look into the things of God; and the mysteries of that kingdom enlarge the reaches of our thought; light from another world illuminates the dark night around us, and shows us the meaning of things which before were to us as a problem that we could not solve. Believe me, to "seek those things which are above," is to clear up many difficulties.

I mention one point more by which we may be enabled to see with more precision what St. Paul means. "Seeking those things which are above" helps us not only to reach towards, but gradually and steadily—I may add unconsciously—*to attain to virtues*, purely Christian. Take the example in this chapter. St. Paul, when finding fault with the Gnostic heresy of Colosse, found fault, in the few verses preceding our text, with a kind of humility. The contrast in his mind here is, of course—the contrast between the false humility of the heretics, and the true humility of the

Christian—the contrast, in short, between affectation and truth. The power of humility, a virtue unknown in the ancient world, is this—that it places the soul under the sway of truth. Affectation—the very reverse of it—was bred by this terrible heresy with which the apostle dealt. But "seek those things which are above;" gaze into that higher world; contemplate the life of God; see the image of Jesus enthroned in glory; enter into the thought of that eternity, into the sphere of which you are born by the regenerating grace of the Spirit, revived by the converting power of God; and then, and then only, be you ever so great in mind, ever so powerful in hand, ever so far-reaching in thought, ever so deep in sympathy, you will realize your nothingness in presence of that supernal glory, and the contemplation of the "things above" will create, or assist in creating, in the soul, *the* virtue of the life of Jesus—the virtue of humility.

So too it is with other virtues; but on this I cannot enlarge to-day. Let me ask you, however, to think at least of this, that if you want to give precision to your efforts in advancing in the Christian life, you must "seek those things which are above;" that if you want to give precision to your thought of those things, you may answer to yourself, "The 'things which are above,' which, if I seek, shall certainly be given, have power to change the tone and temper of my life; to enlarge the reaches of the thought of my mind; to create virtues within me which make me like to my Creator—especially to create the fundamental virtue, the virtue of humility."

Well, it is by giving precision to these vague yearnings of the human heart, to which it supplies an adequate object, that Christianity helps us to advance. St. Paul points further, however, to that truth which gathers all "the things which are above" into one focus, and thereby removes all possible and paralyzing vagueness. He tells us to seek the things that are above, "*where Christ sitteth on the right hand of God.*" It is not only, then, by bringing these "things" before you; it is by gathering up their richest promise and essential attractions into One Who is, at once, an Ideal and an Object that you are enabled to advance. The power of an ideal is to mould character, as the power of a standard is to measure it. The character of Jesus, as it lies before you, sketched in history, is the same, you know, up there in glory, as once it was on earth in sorrow. To "seek the things which are above," *where He sitteth,* is not only to look for gifts and graces, but to gaze on the Uncreated Loveliness and thereby tone your character to that glorious picture.

Yes, He is more than an Ideal: He is an Object. To advance along life—the Christian life—is to advance nearer to Christ. It was so with Paul. He knew Him externally; he accepted His revelations; he took hold of the idea of His character; he learned the truth that had been revealed. But at last he learned to know more, much more, of Christ than could thus be learned. Why? Because, attracted towards that Object of desire, he was advancing. He knew no longer Christ "according to the flesh:" he knew Him in a deeper, in a spiritual sense. To gaze at Him as His likeness is sketched in the Gospels is a great blessing, a great help; but to *feel* His Presence within, as the soul tries to answer to all the touches of His penetrating grace, is to know Him spiritually, and become closer to Him. The power of an advancing life is the seeking indeed these "things above" by willing conformity to the upward impulse of the grace of God, and with the living hope, which Christianity supplies of ultimate attainment; but above all the spring of that life advancing over all parts of the being, in consecration of gifts, use of graces, growth of high thoughts, perfection of desires, is a fixedness of loving gaze on that one central Figure where all find their embodiment and their glorification, the Figure of the enthroned and glorified Jesus, the Ideal of that higher, heavenly life, the Object of the love of the Redeemed.

These are the powers of an advancing Christian life. Now, in closing, what have I to say to you, to apply such words? This. The Christian life is *a life of advance*. It is a life of inner yearnings, purified, strengthened, steadied powers from God. It is a life going on towards an object, to the complete fruition of which it is intended to attain at last. Is it yours?

Are you being contented with holy thoughts for a day or two, a week or two, a moment or two? Are you going on or standing still? Are you content to have had thoughts of God profoundly? Are you content to have been moved by the Spirit earnestly; or are you determined that though you have not yet attained, attain—God helping you—you will?

If it is so, notice what must be your case. It has been said that, in the middle ages, men were inspired by the thought of patriotism—and in our time they are inspired only by the thought of commercial enterprise—that we now forget the thought of country in the engrossing necessity of labour. I do not know whether or not this is precisely true; but I do know that in the Christian life, the sense of personal need, the thought therefore of labour, and the enthusiasm for country must meet and be united.

You will recollect, some of you, an anecdote recorded by one of the greatest of French orators, how one of the wickedest and cruelest of Roman emperors was once startled by the estimate, formed by a prisoner brought before him, of his own place in life. The wretched tyrant, who for years had been amusing himself with the grossest debaucheries and the basest cruelties, was astonished by this stranger whose nationality he could not fix. He was puzzled by the account the man gave of himself. A Roman he was not; a Greek he was not; nor yet a barbarian. What in the world then could he be?

There was an answer upon the man's lips, clear enough to us, though an enigma for Nero: he was a Christian. That truth absorbed him. Neither "Greek nor Jew, barbarian, Scythian, bond nor free," arrested the thought of one who had realized his place in the higher sphere. Above all, he was a Christian. He had realized a fundamental fact: the thought of it was governing his life. My brothers, if you are to advance in the life of glory you must realize and know that fact. Your country is a heavenly one. In the depth of your life nothing you can *do* in the outer world can enter so as to satisfy. But to realize the fact that the crisis has passed over you, that you are in new sphere, that you belong to a heavenly country—that is a thought to urge you onward. "They that say such things declare plainly that they seek a country."

You must go further: St. Paul the apostle, and those to whom he wrote, and whose heresy he battered with his unflinching and pitiless logic, agreed on one point. They agreed that *the* hindrance in the way of all advance was what St. Paul would call "the mind of the flesh." I apprehend he did not mean by this mere sensual appetite; he meant all things that fall below the sphere of our regenerate life. Recollect that, after realizing your place in that sphere, you must be diligent to pluck up and to pull down all that hinders there the advance of the soul. You must recognise the fact St. Paul recognised, that with the "mind of the flesh" there must be a fight without quarter. One step more, and then, indeed, you are on your journey. You must not be negative. You must be positive. You must learn that heaven is your country, and try to live in—not merely think of—heaven, in thought, in aspiration, in desire. Remove the hindrances to this, and place one picture before you, one object towards which to strive. Oh, it must govern your thoughts in your quiet moments. Oh, it must meet your eyes in times of temptation. Oh, it must rule your life by its standard of purity. It must be your ideal of manhood. You must take care to take none but it: take care to take it as such completely—the image of Jesus the Redeemer. To set Him always before you, to think whether you are pleasing Him in what you do, to ask Him for His grace to guide in action; to love those around you because Christ is in them "the hope of glory," to place Him before you not only as your Ideal and Object, but as your final, your complete Reward, and yet to look for Him not in the future only, but now; to seek Him not in heaven, but here; to ask that He may be manifested in your heart, to pray that His spirit permeate your life,—this is to be "seeking those things which are above." And if you do this, if you recognise the fact, that you are in a sphere of immortality—that therefore you must quarrel with, and fight down, and cleave asunder "the mind of the flesh;" if you struggle against it in all its renewed assaults, and, whilst doing so, set before you that sweet picture for daily contemplation, then what is your life? It is *an advance along a journey* that may be infinite, but the joys of which, as you move on, are infinite too. You are leaving the old days of conversion, leaving the first moment of realization, leaving the start of your pilgrimage. Your place in the world may be low, common, and quiet, your mental gifts may be far from dazzling, but your life, your real life, is " shining more and more unto the perfect day."

My brothers, is it so? This is a great reality. To grow in the knowledge of Jesus Christ is a possibility to every soul, young and old. As you do so, your hopes will extend, for when the vision is before you, and you know that you are struggling on, answering to God's grace, nearer and nearer to it, then hope, hope—the "bright hope" "full of immortality"—glorifies and enlightens the dark corners of your poor fading mortal life, and the pressure of the things of time and sense, the anxieties of business, the weariness of labour, the trials of ill-health, the sorrows of others' tempers, the melancholy thoughts that come from bereavement and suffering, these sit lightly on the soul that is advancing, on the soul that has realized that there must be no lagging, no giving way, but, God helping it, an ever onward progress until it is perfected in the likeness of Christ.

Blessed are you if it is so. Blessed are you if you are determined that your life shall be an advancing one, that each day shall bring its lessons, as each day brings its trials and its battles; that each morning Jesus shall be before you; your prayers better said; your Saviour more steadily gazed at; heavenly things more longed for; the spirit of grace more earnestly demanded. Blessed are we if, when all earthly things come at last to be ended; when the trials of life are drawing to a close, when the supreme moment is approaching, and the shadows of death are deepening round us, blessed, if we have not chosen the interests, the pleasures, or the satisfactions of a world fading into the dim distance of the past; but, instead of reputations, successes, or glories, what alone can last for ever—"the things which are above"—those treasures of Eternity—"where Christ sitteth on the right hand of God."

My brothers, have you chosen? I trust you have. Oh then, slack not your effort. Oh then, fail not in your prayers. Oh then, cease not to cry for help. Recollect, you must not be content, until those cryings are satisfied, and they can only be satisfied when you see Him eye to eye, and face to face, and are lost in the glory of that everlasting Presence which here, on earth, you have lived-for and loved so long.

SERMON III.

Christian Watching.

" Watch therefore: for ye know not what hour your Lord doth come."
—St. Matthew xxiv. 42.

RELIGION is the passion of mankind, Religion is the uprising of a strong, and irrepressible desire within the heart of the creature towards the great Creator. Religion has taken many forms; it has shown itself in many shapes. It has suited itself to many nationalities; it has robed itself in many garbs. But religion, whatever form, or shape, or garb it has appeared in, has ever been a passionate longing of the creature towards his Creator.

Now, the revelation of Christ, the faith of Christendom, teaches us this—that when the currents of religious feeling, rushing forth from the heart of humanity, have met with Christ, then, and then only, have they been moulded into really fruitful and permanent forms. If we try to see the outlines of those forms, to bring out in distinctness something of that shadowy mystery of religious temper, one mark of it, at least, is brought before us in such sayings as those of the text.

One word that our Lord uses to characterize religion, to indicate one "note" at least of a sincerely religious mind, is that remarkable word so often repeated in the last days of His life, "Watch!"

The first thing, then, upon which I would fasten your thought is the fact that "watching" is a "note," a characteristic note, of the Christian life. We have thought over *labour*, as Christians look at it, we have considered the *advance* of the soul, as it goes on towards God, and this afternoon I would ask you simply to note the one fact that "*watching*" is a characteristic feature of Christianity.

A fact (I may pause to remind you) it certainly is. Whatever it *means*, at least the naked fact is true. If you look at the last hours of our Lord's life you will find Him perpetually reiterating His exhortation. When He stands on the mount, across the valley over against the Temple of Jerusalem; when He looks at those mighty structures placed there by Herod, making the glory of the old temple vanish into nothing before the fresher splendours of the new; when He sits there gazing over the lordly city in all its pride and life and beauty,—one of the reiterated refrains of His teaching to His apostles is, "Watch therefore."

Last words are solemn words. Last words are fruitful words, for death is the summing-up of life, and the last act of any man is only the final result of the many acts which have preceded it, in his human history. The last words of Jesus witnessed to the current of His thoughts throughout all His earthly life, and among His last words we find none of more frequent repetition than this word, " Watch ! "

It is scarcely needful to prove this statement further from Scripture. If you look through the closing chapters of the Evangelists, if you look through the teachings of St. Paul,—everywhere, up and down his Epistles—if you listen to one of the reiterated teachings of St. Peter as he warns men against the frailty under which he himself had sunk; if you go on to the fainter echoings of the Apostle John from his prison in Patmos, looking down from the height of the glory of God's revelation—everywhere, first and last, my statement is borne out by the testimony of Scripture—a characteristic " note " of Christian life is comprehended in this one word, " Watch ! "

Well, if it is so, let me now try to answer in part —for I shall not attempt, of course, to answer it fully —one question, and to explain the meaning of that answer: the question is, What is Christian watching ? And further, if answered, the meaning of the answer will be made clear by considering what it is that *necessitates* such watching, and lies behind it.

First, then, what is Christian watching ? I have said that I only attempt to answer that question partially. Partially I can answer it by two remarks. First of all, in Christian watching there is implied a *vigorous exercise of a Christian conscience.* My friends, you are all aware that conscience differs, in this respect, from all other judges—that conscience is individual, our consciences do not deal with outside humanity, they deal with *ourselves.* Others may judge, others may blame, but their blame or their judgment passes over us unheeded, sweeps away into the distance of a past that we care not for, as the mist of the mountain sweeps onward before a rising breeze. But there is one judgment that will not pass, that will not be silenced ; one voice that *will* be heard whether it praise or blame, one that comes with something of the force of our Master's own utterances, that speaks to us as Christ speaks: " But *I* say unto *you.*"

Now, conscience is that voice. Conscience distinguishes itself from all judges because it is individual and personal in all its demands and judgments. If it be so, how is it you must exercise it? I answer, first of all, by trying to give it more and more of *a keen perception.* You will agree with me, that the powers of perception are very different in different men. You find one man who takes up the work of a great author, looks carefully over its pages, and as he looks, though his eye glances quickly from line to line, he gathers in all the faintest *nuances,* all the slightest shades of meaning, and his heart is filled with laughter, or with tears. He possesses the power of perception. You meet with another, whom circumstances have placed in some of the greatest historical scenes of which you or I have learned and dreamt since we were born; he stands on the plains of Marathon, where nations met in a death-struggle, and the world's history was changed: he stands on the Roman Campagna, and sees it rolling up and down before him, clothed with flowers, and bathed in a sunlight, all new in its brilliance and splendour to his English eye; he goes to sacred scenes where sacred feet have trodden; he stands on the hill above Athens, and thinks perhaps for a moment, because he has read his Bible, that once Paul stood, and once Paul preached there; but at the end of it all (I speak not from fancy but from experience) he comes home again and simply dilates to you upon the entire absence of agricultural care, or the complete want of commercial enterprise to be found in other parts of Europe as contrasted with England! You feel, when such a man talks to you, that it is useless to argue with him. You feel that, whatever other gifts he has, at least he has not the gift of mental perceptiveness. He has, as we say, *missed the point.*

Now, you and I, when we wish to quicken and increase the power of conscience, must do so by teaching it to be more and more keen in perception. Conscience must stand before us, as a watcher on a ship stands, guiding the bark of the soul through the wild waves and the thick darkness of this deep night of life, and crying out to us, from moment to moment, in the voice of the great Lord Whose echo it is, "What I say unto you, I say unto all, 'Watch.'" To exercise your conscience in keen perception is in part to obey the command to "*watch.*"

But conscience requires more than to be keenly perceptive; it requires also to be wide in its range of vision; it must *omit nothing.* Dear friends, we know well that life is made up of what are called trifles. Life! At times we look at it as a wide arena, with great acts in it; we think of great men, and measure their deeds as man measures greatness; we think of ourselves, and in one sense justly, as being very small in the scale of creation; but we have to remember that wherever there is real greatness—I mean wherever there is greatness whose renown shall ring throughout the courts of Eternity—it has come not from striving to do great deeds, but from striving to do all deeds in a great way. Conscience must learn to omit nothing; must not fret over trifles, but it must not leave them out; it must recollect—it must learn increasingly to recollect—that attention to the little things of every day is an element in that attitude of a Christian which the Lord calls "Watching."

I may notice another way in which you may exercise conscience so as to obey the Lord's command. You must exercise it to assist you in *wise decision.* *Wise* decision, I submit to you, depends, in great measure, upon habit and ability in making a true valuation of consequences. I suppose that the really clever business man in Manchester, if he is wisely to decide upon what step to take in a commercial enterprise, must have carefully valuated consequences; and, in proportion as he is capable of doing so, in that proportion will his decision be, what the world will call, wise; and our Lord has taught us to imitate such action in exercise of a wisdom which is not of this world. Now, conscience, if heeded, if quickened, supplies us with the *data* necessary for a rapid estimate of consequences, and as we practise ourselves in gazing, in quiet moments, on the consequences of life with *its* assistance, it becomes clearer in its statements, more ready and sure, more powerful in the assistance given by it to the will, towards wise decision; and the making of these wise decisions is simply, as the Christian sees, an act of obedience to the Lord's command, " Watch therefore."

Once more; recollect that, if conscience must be keen in vision, if it must omit nothing, if it must be quick and ready in assisting to wisdom in decision, it must also finally and above all things be *peremptory in command*. Conscience *may* be wrong, it *may* make mistakes, but it must never be disobeyed. To disobey conscience is to commit the last disloyalty. It is to learn to be untrue to yourselves. All sins may be condoned but that. If you are untrue to yourselves you must reap terrible consequences. Conscience *will* make mistakes, if you have been careless about educating it; but, mistake or no mistake, its commands are peremptory and it must be obeyed. Certainly it is true that, in this case, *the Christian* has much with which to supplement its forces. I said just now—*Christian* conscience.

My friends, conscience needs *illumination*. It needs the illumination that comes from prayer; it needs the illumination that comes from the Scriptures; it needs the illumination that comes from the wise advice of patient and experienced friends. It needs more, it needs *reinforcement;* it needs the presence of the Lord of conscience; it needs to feed upon the power of Christ, the life of our Divine Redeemer, the one life that can invigorate all our lives; it needs that you should seek Him, both in prayer, and in those Divine means of most intimate intercourse where you and I can meet and embrace Him,—in the sacraments of the Christian Church. Illuminate conscience, reinforce conscience, educate conscience as well as you can, but recollect that, in the last resort, it is a peremptory judge, that it is better to obey it, mistaken even if it be in some degree, than to disobey it and run the risk of thereby passing over a judgment, the nearest representative for us of the judgment of God.

You may say to me, when I urge you to this exact and earnest obedience, that I am virtually asking you to precipitate yourselves, at any rate sometimes, into the gulf of sheer loss. Certainly at times it may appear to be a loss to obey our conscience. Such an array of authorities against it!—public opinion in all its pomp of accumulated judgments, the wise counsels of men whom we value and respect, undeniably based upon a wider experience than that of our single conscience, and warning us against a quixotic choice of loss when all the time we might be advancing towards gain. These indeed are forces difficult to resist.

My friends, in the last days of those cities which were overwhelmed by the floods of lava from the fierce fires of Vesuvius—in the days when Pompeii was passing into her living grave—men tell us (the story has been disputed, and I do not vouch for its accuracy) that the Roman soldiers took their places at the gates of the doomed city, and unflinchingly maintained their position whilst the floods of death were pouring over them. Was it altogether loss if so they did? Was it altogether loss, if with pale face and steadied foot each held his ground amidst the most frightful forces of overwhelming nature? I am sure it was not. Courage and loyalty are never lost. Such conduct must enrich the records of history, and the experience of the human race, with the fruitful thought of the power of a splendid discipline, the ennobling thought of the possibility and greatness of an unflinching obedience.

You and I remember an old story, one that made an impression upon us, perhaps, in boyhood, the story of the loss of the Birkenhead. You remember how the British soldiers, with the calm sea, and the quiet setting sun, stood shoulder to shoulder upon the deck of the vessel that was steadily "settling down," and would not move —not a man of them—from their places, till the weak and helpless were carried to the shore. Do you think it was altogether loss, that those brave men, of our flesh and blood and nationality, sank down into waters on a calm, quiet summer evening without giving one shriek of horror, without moving one step from their ranks? It was not. The thought of that magnificent heroism, the thought of that obedience to duty, the thought wakened by the last ringing cheer, that rose from the dying hearts of brave British soldiers, as they sank into a watery grave, penetrated at that time into the living hearts of men and women, ay and of boys who read or heard of it, and has never been forgotten to this day. It worked its work. It was not sheer loss. Duty done is never sheer loss. Self-interest demands something else, but, believe me, you and I live in a world of eternity, and the passing conditions of a passing time are no measurement of the final effects of that which is done by a being that shall live for ever. Conscience may demand of you what *appears* to be sheer loss, but, be sure of it, in the long run, if you obey its judgment, if you exercise it in such judgments, if you question it to assist you in wise decision, if you train it by the illuminations of grace, by the warnings of Scripture or experience; then you are going far on the path that the Lord indicates as the path of a Christian:

"Watch therefore: for ye know not what hour your Lord doth come."

There is another point in Christian "watching" which I must note. It is not only by the exercise of conscience: it is by a *patient practice of thoughtfulness*. You will remember, perhaps, some of you, the old formulary of the great French philosopher: "I think, therefore I am." You will recollect also, what has been truly said about that formulary by a careful thinker of modern England, —that *that* philosopher who framed it was not arguing, in a false way, from a gratuitous assumption as his premise to a conclusion, but was simply stating a fact;— that personality, or personal life, was not proved by, but consisted in, consciousness; that whilst the form of our consciousness never changes the matter is ever changing; or, to put it in less philosophical, and more common, English,—our emotions and feelings and acts of will are ever passing. They sweep away like figures in a dream, but *we* remain. You and I have had emotions this last week, perhaps have committed acts of our will, or have had thoughts in our minds, which have died away into the dim distance of a far fading past; but take the inner self, the conscious self, and make it to exercise itself on these variable forms, to seize emotion and to "precipitate" it into some definite shape; to take thought and make it pass into a permanent form; to lay hold upon will and make it act in one definite direction—to do that is to set the life sweeping onward, like a resistless current, in one direction; it is to place the whole soul in one steady attitude; and this definite directing of the current of life, and this steady fixing of the attitude of soul—this, and nothing else, is what our blessed Redeemer calls. "*watching.*" "What I say to you I say to all, Watch." "Watch therefore: for ye know not what hour your Lord doth come."

And now I ask you practically, Do you practise thoughtfulness? You say your prayers. Ah, but do you *think*, as you say them, what it is you need all day! You speak to God about your grave necessities, about the virtues that you require. But do you *think*, "This day I shall be tried," and do you patiently set the current of your life against the object which you are determined to sweep away, if you are to live for God? You go to church; you listen to a sermon, you like or dislike it; you hear the words of Holy Scripture. But do you *think* carefully, quietly, patiently, as accurately as you can, over such truth as God has brought to your soul, in that reading of Scripture, or that discourse, that you may turn it to *practical* effect? I counsel you to practise thoughtfulness. Half the sins of half the world spring from thoughtlessness. You take for granted what you ought humbly but earnestly to examine. You act on bad principles because they are common, and therefore, without thinking, you suppose they must be true. O young men and young women, with life upon you strong, and passions powerful, recollect that many a sin which darkens your understanding, stains your imagination, chills your emotions, lowers your life, is simply the outcome of a wretched thoughtlessness. "*Watch ye therefore: for ye know not what hour your Lord doth come.*"

I said to you in starting (and I must fulfil my promise) that I would not only try to point out to you some duties of watchfulness,—*that* I have now endeavoured to do; but that I would also try to indicate on what they rest. What *necessitates* watchfulness?

Well, I must answer briefly, what necessitates this characteristic of Christian life is, that there are unchanging facts underlying variable forms in the continuous battle that is raging between good and evil. These I may indicate in two ways—by looking at both the contending powers. Evil is ever varying in its expression, but it is continually the same in its essential conditions. In old times it came out among the Romans, for instance, in the form of barbaric carelessness about human life. The Greeks, by their contempt for everything except beauty of form, and philosophic thought, showed an indifference to the deeper moral principles of a higher life.[1] In our own days, in Eastern Europe (where all our eyes are fixed for the moment, where all our hearts have been turned through so many months), we have seen from time to time—although we have been in

[1] Preached at the time when England was shocked by accounts of Turkish atrocities in Bulgaria.

great doubt and hesitancy as to what was the true solution of our difficulties—we have seen multiplied indications of a similar carelessness of life, and more than carelessness; of the utmost, the most brutal cruelty, of the almost organized lust, which has ever characterized the rule of the Eastern barbarians, from the time when, under the successors of the false prophet, they first invaded the civilization of Europe. Different forms indeed have shrouded the same power, but the same power—the power of evil—has ever been lurking behind. In our own days, and in our own country, it is precisely the same. Here we have certain social compacts whereby evil works out its ends, though in less distinctly repulsive forms. We have our Divorce Courts, breaking down the old sanctity of that indissoluble bond, which human law may pretend to tear, but which remains indissoluble none the less. Here we have our commercial schemes, turning out too often to be mere acts of Commercial Dishonesty, and, in the great cities of England, helping to undermine the moral principles of young men in their trials to earn their livelihood, as so many have to do here in Manchester; shaking the foundation of our credit in the far-off regions of the world; turning our vaunted civilization into a handy method for spreading a spiritual plague. Here we have, in fact, various social expressions, changing from moment to moment, of the one unchanging power of evil.

And besides all that, you have the power of evil

expressed not only in social compact, but also under literary guise! We, as a literary nation, an educated people, laying great stress too upon education, are entrapped into the grasp of evil by that very literary enterprise which we respect so much. You take up the serial literature of the day, and you find abundance of it to be simply moral or spiritual poison; much of it inspires the young mind with polluting thoughts, disgraceful imaginations, and base or unbelieving principles. True it is, thank God, that England at this moment possesses a literature which she can be proud of before the world; but, true though *that* is, let us remember that upon the drawing-room tables of London or of Manchester, there lie such expressions of literary power as are, only under a changed garb, expressions of the old enemy—of the unwearied power of evil.

Further, I remind you of this: that in the day we live in, the contest with evil becomes particularly difficult from a new feature in it. Once men recognised a fact now ignored or denied; once they believed in the personality of the tempter. A very spirited, a very able, a very cultured writer of the day, whose writings have had no inconsiderable influence over the minds of the young men in Cambridge and in Oxford—I hope, and I believe, NOT of the young men in Manchester—tells us amidst much, as I think, frivolous trifling, something of this sort,—that Satan is a mere shadow, thrown by the guilt and terror of the human mind. When one sees such opinions prevailing, one is witness to the latest triumph of Satan, his success in persuading men in our days, to deny his personality altogether. My friends, beneath the varying forms and shows of evil there lurks an energetic propaganda, there lies the power of one who possesses vast science, keen perception, long experience; and who has exercised that power to such effect that he has persuaded men that he himself is not.

The one great fact ever to be remembered in the contest with evil is this, that under varying forms its subtlety, malignity, and power are the same; that the same energy is ever exerted; and that you and I—just because the form varies, and because behind it there is ever the same fearful personal foe—have a need, in the Christian life, of that attitude of conscience, that practice of thoughtfulness, which our Divine Redeemer calls *watching*. "Watch therefore: for ye know not what hour your Lord doth come."

There is the other side of the battle, in it also an unchanging fact which our dear Lord most distinctly indicates in the text. If it be true that evil is varying in form, and always energetic in action, what of the other side? Simply this: God is ever judging it. Oh remember it, that is the reason for watching. God has judged, and is judging, and will judge evil. God does it, not because He is capricious, but because it is a necessity of His glorious nature. He were not God if He did not judge, and because He is ever judging, you and I must "watch." For the safety of the soul depends on this: it depends upon its energetic action alongside of God, upon its keen watching to see *how* God is judging, and its determination to take its stand by the side of its Creator, from Whom it comes, to Whom it goes. God judges in three ways. He will one day through the one Mediator. "There is one Mediator between God and man, the man Christ Jesus." God's action on humanity is ever through that One, for that One is God.

(1) Well, first, God judges evil *now*, in His providential action, upon our lives. The providences of God are clear before us, if we look. By His Providence, His laws are worked out. "As a man sows, *so* shall he reap." If you sow wheat, you cannot reap barley. If you sow to the flesh, you cannot reap to the spirit; if you sow to corruption, you cannot reap to everlasting life. The Providence of God teaches this—that our final, our ultimate benediction, depends upon our sincere and earnest service to Himself. Again, the Providence of God speaks through opportunity. Opportunities! We see them across the hills of life; we beckon to them to come, and they come to us; they come with pale and doubting faces; they carry to us great gifts which we may use or may abuse. We look at them for a moment—and we pass them by. Some pleasure has arrived, more beautiful, more persuasive, and opportunity of good is gone. But opportunity has left its message, and its message is

always the same as every other witness of the providence of God. God, by His providence in your heart, God by the opportunities of your life, is judging evil—that right is right and wrong is wrong—and His creature, because so He is judging, and because the Lord is coming, in that providence, in those opportunities, must be ever " watching."

(2) Need I say that He judges it also in His final coming? Ah, you may think that that coming of Jesus which lies before us, is altogether distinct in character from those providences and opportunities of God. My brothers, my sisters, it is not. The coming of Jesus is according to the laws of God. God works according to law, and law works itself out into decisive crises. The final crisis of humanity will only be a gathering up of all the crises of God's providential and opportune workings, which have gone before. Jesus comes in providence; Jesus comes in opportunity; Jesus will come in the final judgment to gather up all the judgments that He has delivered before. He told His disciples it would be so, as He sat on the hill over against Zion. They scarcely believed it, but soon they learned it—learned it by the fate of the Holy City, which was a type of the fate of the world. All the workings of the Roman empire, confronting the rebellious spirit of the Jewish nation, had been gathering themselves up to a crisis. Nero—so it would appear from St. Paul—was to be a chief actor in the drama of the destruction of Jerusalem;

yet Nero did not appear personally in the final catastrophe. The last act was done by Titus, but Titus was carrying out the designs of Vespasian, and Vespasian, in turn, owed his appointment to Nero. And so the great action, begun in the wicked emperor, passed on to its fulfilment, by steady progress, because the laws of God's judgment are constant, when evil is working against the righteousness of God. The overthrow of Jerusalem was a witness of *the* final overthrow—a great, a true, an accurate witness—because God's judgments *eventually*, are like God's judgments *then* and *now*. God judges us, I say, in providence and opportunity. He will judge us also when Christ shall come. "Watch therefore, for ye know not what hour" Providence speaks, "what hour" opportunity comes, "what hour" the last Providence shall decree the final breath that marks the close of your earthly existence, "what hour" the last opportunity that shall forewarn you, that Christ is coming in the clouds of glory. Watch therefore!

(3) Does He judge otherwise, otherwhere? He does. I have spoken to you of the *present*, which is Providence; I have spoken to you of the *future*, which is the coming of Jesus. O my brothers, my sisters, there was a judgment in the *past*, which, this week, I cannot omit to remind you of, for it is specially a judgment *now*. He judged evil in the Passion of His sorrow. On the Cross there was the throne of judgment. You and I have entered on Passion-tide; we are nearing the Holy

Week; we are coming to the fringe of the dark clouds that enfold in their dusky drapery our suffering Redeemer; is it possible the working of business, is it possible the trifles of pleasure, is it possible the little things of daily life, can so engross all your attention, and drag down all your energies, that you will not fix your concentrated efforts, the whole strain and stress of your mind and heart, upon the sufferings of the Divine Redeemer?

To meditate upon the sufferings of Jesus, to keep your Holy Week, to observe your Good Friday, to enter upon Passion-tide as a Christian should enter upon it, what is it to do? It is to "watch" *with* Jesus. "Could ye not watch with Me one hour?" said He to His disciples. "Can ye not watch with Me one fortnight, one week, one day?" says He to the people of Manchester. Will ye not do it? It is more than to watch with Him. It is to learn the judgments of God; it is to see the meaning, the blackness, the eternal horror, the final destruction, of evil; the brilliant beauty, the splendour, the glory, of high principle, noble effort, truth of conscience, purity of love, earnestness of desire—longing for, and reaching up to, the presence of God. Such is the Passion of Jesus, in its teaching for us all.

O loved Redeemer! O Lord of Glory! may He give us grace to enter upon that Passion, that we may hate the evil and love the good; that we may rise to a more quickened conscience and deeper thoughtfulness; seeing that, whenever He meets us—in the memory of His Passion, in the opportunities of His providence, or in the final catastrophe of His judgment—we shall always have needed the characteristic teaching of a Christian's life: "Watch therefore: for ye know not what hour your Lord doth come."

If then you will practically watch, you must have earnest and eager thoughts after God; you must be raising your minds into that eternity, where you and I are living, and which we so often forget. Oh, life is full of trifles; life is overlaid with what is merely transient; but we are born in a sphere of being which is everlasting. Let your thoughts of God be earnest and yearning, in the midst of your work. If you are to watch you must go further. You must not be content with an easy assumption that *probably* what *you* are doing and what *you* like is *the will of God*. You must be desirous to *know* it. You must pray to see it. You must strip yourself more and more of the adventitious covering of opinion, or the passing applause of the hour, that may stay you from seeking *it*. You must go straight on, through the dimness and darkness, asking Him: "My God, let me work, or let me be idle; only let Thy will be done." That would be to "watch."

Go one step more—and then I have done. You must not only have these eager and earnest thoughts of God, not only be struggling to know His will accurately, as He reveals it. No; you cannot do one, you cannot do the other, unless you have before you an object. Strip from the Christian life personal affection, take from it individual devotion, and you have left it an arid desert, you have left it a miserable mistake. There is one way by which you and I are called on, in our watching; one way by which we are enabled to be real sentinels, one way by which we can act as true soldiers: it is by placing that crucified Form before us, it is by "looking unto Jesus, the Author and Finisher of our faith."

O my brothers, do you watch *with* Jesus? Do you look *to* Jesus? Is your desire that your life may be shaped on that Model? Is your yearning that you may attain to the union with your one dear Lord? Blessed are ye if so it is. Your hands may fall down, your heart may be faint and weary; but oh, He will be near you to quicken you in your energies and efforts. *He* is the Giver of all grace, to help you. *He* will crown you at last, for He is coming. Years are passing; life is failing; death is near. You and I must stand at our post, looking out into the darkness, making each trifle tell upon eternity, and then, we shall be ready with joyful anticipations, for we shall be living as Christians should be living, following the teachings and using the strength that comes from Christ.

Oh, look to Him for that strength, pray for courage to be faithful to His teaching, and ask (He will grant it) for His benediction upon your toil. Try to watch *with* Him, and then you may watch *by* Him. Pray to

Him that He may help you, and indeed He will; you cannot watch unless your Lord, Who is coming, enables you; but if He enables you, then, indeed, you can—ay! and to the end.

> "Thou the grace of life supplying,
> Thou the crown of life wilt give ;
> Dead to self, and daily dying,
> Life of life, by Thee we live."

SERMON IV.

Christian Battle.

"Thou therefore endure hardness, as a good soldier of Jesus Christ."
—2 TIMOTHY ii. 3.

THE Apostle Paul, in this exhortation—an exhortation which he delivered to the young and deeply beloved son in Christ, whom he himself had consecrated to the episcopate of the Church—puts before us another view of the Christian life. Whatever may have been the cause that led St. Paul to speak in this particular *way*, whether it was that he was so intimately acquainted with the military movements of the empire, at the time of his imprisonment—from the fact that he was brought into constant and intimate contact with the soldiers of the Prætorian guard—or not, at any rate we are quite sure of this, that it was an aspect of the Christian life which perpetually presented itself to his mind; and if we stand for a moment, as St. Paul seems to stand, and gaze down upon that scene on which are constantly gazing the "great cloud of witnesses," catalogued by himself probably, in another of his Epistles; if we look on the striking panorama that stretches before us, and the main features of which we have been trying to discern, and to photograph, from different points of view this Lent, we find most certainly that, whatever else the Christian life means, we are forced to acknowledge, as we watch the gradual development of human history, modified and conditioned by the application to it of Christian principles, that *that* life is a *life of battle*.

We are trying to look, as you know, at the Christian life from different standpoints, in order to acquire something like a comprehensive idea of its requirements; in order, by taking a survey of it, first from here and then from there, to form a more accurate estimate of what, after conversion, it means; that is, what are some of the leading conditions of the spiritual life of any man, from the point of time when he has given himself consciously, and thoroughly, to God.

Well, to-day I view the Christian life as a *life of battle*. We have considered it as a *life of labour*, we have remembered that we ought to be *advancing*. We have not forgotten that the life that we are leading is a *life of watching;* let me remind you now of a further feature in Christianity, that, step by step, as we are advancing, however laborious, however watchful we be, our way will be contested.

Now, first of all, if you look at the text you will notice, that the apostle is putting before us a plain exhortation to conduct, based upon a distinct statement of position. The position he states to be this: "as a soldier"—the conduct, "endure hardness;" and when we come to examine into the necessity of such conduct, based upon the exigencies of such a position, we are thrown back upon the old thought of the enemy with whom we have to contend—that enemy, to glance at whom is to recognise none other than the old and formidable antagonist, laid under a lasting anathema in our baptismal promises, the one whose friendship we consciously forswore when we learned our catechisms,—the threefold foe united in a triple alliance against our souls: we have, in fact, to fight against the devil, the world, and the flesh.

When we speak of fighting with Satan there is this always to be remembered, that the war has to be waged with one possessed of all the three chief faculties which go to make any malignant power oppressive to a struggling heart: for Satan is undoubtedly possessed, first of all, of natural capacity; secondly, of a wide-reaching science; and thirdly, of a large experience. That is to say, in short words, he possesses, first of all, what belongs to him by his angelic *nature;* secondly, what he has acquired by using the faculties of that nature; and thirdly, the stores which he has accumulated by applying those faculties to the acts of life within the range of his wide opportunities, from the time when that life began in angelic splendour till this moment, when it continues under conditions of utter and overwhelming ruin. But I would remind you further, that Satan, in his fight against us, is seconded by that power within us, which from its intimate connection with our animal organism, and the grovelling direction of all its tendencies, can best be epitomized in its character as "the flesh." I mean by that power, the rising up of our natural desire beyond its proper limitations—the exercise of what is in us, in itself not bad, but practised to a degree, and in a plane where it ought not to find its exercise, whereby it becomes a traitor in the camp, making conditions with the external enemy. And these two enemies, we have to remember also, are reinforced by a third. If "the flesh" is a traitor who makes a concordat with Satan, "the world" is an enemy equally fierce and infinitely more subtle, which acts as a power of reinforcement supplying whatever deficiencies in the contest the others may feel.

"The world:" I need not stop to define it, for you and I—some of us—thought of it not very long ago, and endeavoured to take its accurate measurements. But "the world," in a word, we know, means this: the accumulated force of certain principles sin-born, and sin-strengthened, which tend to undermine the spiritual life. When we come, then, to look at the enemy before us, we see the force of a triple alliance. We see the power of a personality, endowed with all that makes a creature formidable; we see that personality helped by a secret league with a traitor; and we see both reinforced by an external, and almost more mysterious power than either, which we cannot define, or can only define in a fashion approximate to its meaning. Place all these together, and we are confronted with the deadly enemy with whom we have to fight in the struggle for everlasting life.

Now, on a former occasion—for I must not pause upon the mere *fact* now—we tried to recollect that the enemy in himself was always essentially the same, but the expression of the enmity continually varying; the character constant, the expression changeful. Well then, let me remind you, a little more carefully, what the *character of the enemy* is. If we are to see to what course of conduct the apostle would lead us, what the position he assumes as being ours, we must note that character. Well, I do so by marking three features. First of all, in each member of this formidable alliance, there is the exercise of *craft*. Now, by *craft* might first be meant, the delicate skill shown by any in the performance of work; but speaking morally, "craft,"—or here call it "craftiness"—implies that skill is exercised with unworthy cunning; it hints at some deception, it means not only the exercise of any power to attain with precision the object before it, but its exercise under appearances such as to conceal its own true character, and what that object really is.

Now, the character of our enemy is of this sort: the character of one who comes forward in disguise, and, under that disguise, exercises a power altogether different in itself and in its object from what it *appears* to be: that is one feature in the character. And another is this. You and I, if we are to be won away from our position, must be won, not merely by a power disguised, but by a power which, up to a certain point, *does* meet our wants; that is, the main characteristics of the enemy that we have to contend with are—subtlety and seductiveness.

There is about this triple alliance a power, not *of disguising* only its own inner and essential life, but of meeting our needs up to a certain point, and that, just in matters in which those needs are most felt by us all. Man, my brothers, desires two things—beauty and pleasure. If we are to succumb to the attraction of anything, there must be about it some sort of beauty. If we are to rest in any fancied satisfaction, the source of that satisfaction must offer us at least the promise of pleasure; and so, to win you or me over to the deadly enemy, that deadly enemy must not only disguise its own essential character, but it must also have a power of seductiveness overcoming our suspicion or fear of evil, by attracting us with at least the appearance of beauty, and soothing us by the promise of pleasure.

To complete my meaning, and express that character, let me add that not only there must be craftiness, and the power of seduction, but also patient persistence in recurrent and well-timed attack. Men may be attacked once, and they may be scared if the attack is too long continued. Souls constantly say that, in their coldest moments, they are often least disturbed by temptation; and the secret of it is simply this, that when you or I have gone to a certain extent in obedience to Satan, or the world, or the flesh, Satan, the world, and the flesh—the two latter, so to speak, in obedience to the former—will leave us alone for a time, so that the first attack may have its full power of play upon us, and that we may not be placed on our guard by another following it too soon.

The third feature, then, of the character of the enemy is, that there is in it a habit of well-timed and recurrent attack.

Now, however, let me remind you, in passing, that whilst it is folly of the worst kind to attempt, on the one hand, to disguise from ourselves the reality, or to minimize the strength, of the forces opposed to us, lest we become careless and over-confident of victory; on the other, it is equally dangerous so to forget the powers which stand around us as the "mountains around Jerusalem," as to lose sight of the certainty of recurrent assistance, and so yield to the seductions of evil from a craven fear of ultimate defeat. It is one of the enemy's most favourite stratagems to lead us into one or the other mistake. It has ever been so; and a fatal mistake it is. If a great commander cannot overcome an enemy by force, he will try to throw him off his guard by subtle *artifices* and seductions. In the protracted struggle between the armies of the later Empire and the immense hordes of Goths and Alemanni that poured upon them on the Danube and the Rhine, whilst successes and defeats had alternated in the struggle of two Roman emperors, it was by consummate genius and keen astuteness that Theodosius brought about a final capitulation. "A work of prudence rather than of valour," says the historian of the "Decline and Fall,"—if I rightly remember. Had the barbarians been at first less over-confident, and then more united, watchful, and hopeful, they could have overwhelmed the weakened forces of Rome. The emperor had tried the power of constantly recurring attack, and that against a divided enemy; and at length it was by the arts of seduction that the barbarous chief was won over. "I now beheld what I never could believe," said he, "the glories of this stupendous capital!" The surrender of the Gothic chief is not unlike the surrender of the unwary Christian, first over-presuming and neglectful, and then dispirited by ever-recurring attacks, and allured by the enemy's arts of seduction.

For, my friends, remember, there is a city more magnificent in appearance, more alluring in its attractiveness, than the splendid capital of early Eastern Christendom —the city of the world. St. Augustine, in a well-known passage of the "De Civitate Dei,"[1] interprets for us its mysterious attraction, and unveils its real dreadfulness. Two opposing affections—according to this great father

[1] De Civitate Dei, lib. xiv. cap. xxviii.

—contend for mastery over man; the city of the world is the creation of the triumph of one, the celestial country the result of the victory of the other. The one is the love of self, the other is the love of God; but the ultimate ending of one and the other is inevitable. If love for God reaches at last to contempt of self, so love for self must finally attain to contempt for God. The soul seeing the attractive glitter of the city of Evil, would be repelled, if it saw its actual misery; the soul making self, not God, its centre, would be shocked if at once it realized the result. It is an art of the enemy to conceal from us necessary consequences. Over-confidence may throw us off our guard; then recurrent attack may weaken and dismay, then seductive splendour will attract; but if in weakness we yield to the seduction the ultimate issue must be complete catastrophe.

Now, how are we to meet an enemy of so formidable a kind? Well, St. Paul says, "As a soldier." Let me ask you, shortly, to think of some of the features of what he understands by that character. You and I must *fight*, my brothers, must still *fight*, even after our conversion, against the uprising forces of the world, the flesh, and the devil. How are we to act *as soldiers?* Can we grasp at all what is meant by the apostle?

Surely we can. First of all, and essentially, at the root of the soldier-life of a Christian is this—it is a life *of faith.* Dear brothers, think what you mean by the force of faith. Faith for each one, remember, is an *illuminative faculty,* faith is not a mere upspringing of the mind towards a distant Christ. Faith is a *power of the soul* which shows you Eternity as clearly as the power of your eyes which shows you the visible world. There are two things that it is essential, in our battle, to understand—Sin and Virtue: sin is an object of faith; so is virtue. We cannot understand sin except by Divine faith. From the use merely of ordinary natural faculties, we fall into mistakes about sin. We meet men in the world, for instance (to borrow an illustration from a spiritual writer), who have about them a charm of character, a readiness of address, a power of humour, which overcomes us immediately we meet them; we admire them, and yet we know, when we exercise Divine faith, that there may be (for all the merely natural attractiveness) certain features in the inner lives of these very men that are altogether hateful to Almighty God. The natural faculty, of course, does not discern this; it can exercise itself only upon what belongs to nature; the illuminative faculty *of* the faith of the soldier shows him the *danger of sin.*

It is the same with virtue. It is all very well to argue with young men that they *ought* to be virtuous; it is all very well to tell them that "honesty is the best policy," and telling them *that,* of course you tell them the truth,—but, O my brothers, if you and I are to *grasp* the fact, and to make it a principle of life, we need not to be *told* it merely: we have to *learn* it by a Divine power from God. Virtue, in its beauty, is discerned by faith. It has ever been so, even in its highest examples. What was the highest reach of virtue? The life of Jesus of Nazareth. To see virtue in its full blaze of splendour, holiness in its perfect beauty, you must gaze on the Redeemer. I ask you, Did men *understand* Him? I answer, Certainly they admired. From one end of history to the other, a great chorus of admiration rises when we name the Name of our Redeemer. "Admiration," yes, but not full appreciation. It is possible to *admire* what plays on the outside of a beautiful object, without fully appreciating the forces that throw out that exquisite external expression. It is possible to *admire* the breeze-blown spray of the waves of ocean, or its "myriad twinkling smile," or the magic sparkling of phosphorescent light, tossed up like a fringe of fire, from moment to moment in the summer nights, by the action of the vessel as she passes athwart the dancing waves; possible to do all this, without appreciating the marvellous machinery which nature is ever plying to produce such magic spectacles. It was so in the life of Jesus. My friends, there are men in the world who have admired, but who have never been the least capable of appreciating, that life—men who, simply because they could not but admire, have actually cursed. "*Ecrasez l'infame*," was the famous phrase of Voltaire, the acute leader of French scepticism, not that his eyes were shut to that majestic virtue, but that that majestic virtue—as it did not subdue, because in its inner essence he could not appreciate it—still advanced upon him a claim so imperious, that, since submit he would not, there remained only the resource of rebellion. To understand high virtue in any man—pre-eminently in Jesus—requires some exercise of spiritual faculty; in the highest questions, such as this, there must be some exercise of the faculty of faith. · There is needed then, my friends, to see the beauty of holiness, and to understand the terribleness of sin, *the illuminative power of faith.* You must use this faculty, if you are to meet your enemy, as St. Paul says, "as a soldier."

And again, Faith does more than illuminate in the battle. Faith is a dominant faculty: it rules. The great apostle himself, with the memories of the Roman Prætorium pressing upon him, with the thought of that grand organization and those all but invincible armies, penetrating his mind from the experience of his captivity—the great apostle himself speaks of bringing all things into "the *obedience* of faith." Faith is a dominant faculty. It tells a man where his thought may reach to; where it must stop. It draws the frontier line between time and eternity, and, drawing that frontier line, it helps him to act "as a soldier." It is a *divine* capacity which enables the mind to distinguish the *essential* from the *accidental,—essential* joy and beauty, from *accidental* veils and accompaniments of sorrow:—to reach up for what God gives. It is not the exercise of mere opinion.

You and I are living in an age when men, in a sort of seductive way, are perpetually inviting us to strike first one and then another article out of the creeds of Christendom. We are, practically, told that we are in a time when advanced culture, powerful thought, even the progress of mechanical discovery, have put men so completely in possession of the universe they live in, that they can dispense to a great extent with the unseen. We are, in effect, asked to put away all that stops the way of pride and passion; but, oh remember, in your battle of life this is fatal, and *faith* refuses it all. To accept a part of God's revelation, because it commends itself to your *opinion*, is not the exercise of *faith*. Faith is a divine faculty which grasps that which is revealed, on the authority of God, without criticising the substance of such revelation. To take one part of the revelation of God, and turn out another, is, in fact, to reject it all, because you are rejecting just what *you* mislike or misunderstand, and retaining just what *you* choose; and to accept God's revelation rightly, is to bow, in disciplined obedience, on *all* points to God's authority; in fact, to exercise *faith*, "as a soldier." "The whole counsel of God"—to accept it in its entirety, however difficult, mysterious, or opposed to our natural wishes—that is the exercise of the dominant faculty of faith.

If you ask what contribution faith can make to the

equipment of a Christian soldier, I answer it supplies the inspiring principle of *courage*. Courage! My brothers, why is it you are *overthrown* in your wrestling? Why do you act dishonestly? Why do you act impurely? Why is it that you fall back when you are so far advanced? Is not the fact to be explained by this— that you have been playing the coward? Afraid of the voice of men, afraid of the opinion of the crowd, afraid of the sneer of a companion? What is the faculty that inspires us with courage? Faith is that faculty; for it means a venture, and to make a venture, to throw overboard what you love, trusting simply in Him Who says He will give far more—far better to replace it—to do that, is to exercise courage, a courage which springs from bringing into play the faculty of faith. As a soldier, to "endure hardness" is, first of all, the exercise of a *divine faith*.

Further, in opposition to certain features of the character of the enemy, it is also to act with *simplicity*. The world supposes that *simplicity* (to use a common expression, the appositeness of which must be my apology for using it)—the world supposes that simplicity "does not pay." The world supposes (and acts upon its supposition), that everything must be done by craft and policy, that you must not go *direct* to your end. O my brothers, do not believe it. Believe this, that simplicity will bring you into trouble; believe this, that simplicity will cause you difficulty; that it will also, not improbably, give you pain. Many a time you will find, if you act simply, that you will be supposed to be acting in exactly the reverse fashion. Never care. Recollect that the point for the Christian soldier to remember, is to keep his eye steadily fixed upon his Commander, and to meet the forces of the enemy with the only forces that can adequately in the long run overthrow them. Now, if craft is to be met, if that terrible, subtle, renewed attack of Satan is to be resisted, it must be met, it must be resisted, by divine faith; and it must be met, it must be resisted, with simplicity, for God's way alone is the way of victory, and simplicity is part of the character of God. It means being one's simple better self; and when you learn to act simply, with truth to yourself, in the divine life, it means to act as Christ; for to be in a supernatural life, is to be one with Christ, and Christ with you; and when I ask you to act with simplicity, to speak the direct truth, nor fear the consequences, I ask you, in fact, to exert the power of the divine life within you, which is the very presence of our most dear Redeemer. Act simply, "as a soldier."

One point more, in the character of a soldier: if you are to meet your enemy successfully, act *with patience.* The attacks of the world, the flesh, and the devil are recurrent attacks, as I have reminded you just now. How are you to meet them? By patience. Patience is, indeed, a part of faith. "Faith" is a comprehensive term for many virtues which lie enshrouded beneath it.

There are virtues, like the sweet flowers of spring which lie underneath the wide branches of the spreading tree, that they may be sheltered from the strong rays of the fierce sun. That spreading tree is Faith, and those sweet flowers are virtues that grow beneath the shade of its divine extension. My friends, amongst those flowers is patience. Patience, again, is love exerting itself to resistance. Patience does not mean an energy put forth to invade the country of the foe. It means the energy of love in action, that kind of action, and that only, which is implied in resistance. You know what intense power there is in a steady, an unflinching resistance; intense, because concentrated; you know how you eventually must win your way, if I may be pardoned the paradox, simply by standing your ground. It is certain that one of the greatest powers of Christian heroism has been the power of patience. It has always been so, and if the Christian, as a soldier, needs simplicity and faith to fight his battle; certainly not less, but more, he needs also a steady and unflinching patience. I suppose that is one of the reasons why the Church teaches us to pray to God when we are commemorating the Lord's Passion, that we may have something of His perfect patience, as well as of His "great humility," because it is one of the most powerful forces of His human character, strengthened and reinforced by His divine life. Be patient. Ah, my brothers! you cannot conquer without that. Morning after morning, prayers will have to be said. Day after day, you will have to stand firmly against the ridicule, the jest, and the slander. Year after year, even if for a moment the sun of brighter prosperity shine upon you, you have to be prepared for the darkling clouds of stern adversity. You must be exercising patience. Think of the apostle's warning; think of his exhortation. Act in the spirit in which he urged his son in Christ to act, " as a soldier."

Well, if such be some of the features of the soldier's character, what does it all amount to? It amounts, I submit, in practice to precisely what the apostle said, viz. to "enduring hardness." For by "hardness" St. Paul does not mean that you should be callous; that you should not *feel* the power, and the darts of the enemy; he does not mean that the natural humanity within you, should be so shrunk up that you have no appreciation of the danger, nor any sensibility to pain. No, but he means that such virtues should be *exercised* by you with unbending resolution —the divine faith that embraces all those others, the simplicity and the patience which are enwrapped in the faith—that you may be able to present to the enemy a front so decided, so impervious to his assaults, so impossible for him to break, against which he must dash himself in vain, that the determined, unflagging, self-forgetful manner of exercising such powers, may be strictly described as "the enduring of hardness."

Yes, many a young man has had to " endure hardness"

in his ordinary life. He has had to "set his face like a flint," as Joseph set his, when summoned to surrender to a powerful temptation of the flesh. He has had to "set his face like a flint," as you may have to set yours, when you are confronted by a temptation in commercial enterprise, by untruth, or laziness, or dishonesty; and you can only "set your face like a flint," not by an absence of natural sensibility within you, not by the impossibility of your experiencing pain, but by the divine faith that looketh unto Jesus, and the simplicity and the patience which are drawn, for exercise, out of the richly furnished storehouse of His matchless life. That is to "endure hardness as a soldier."

O my brothers, if you think what it is you have to fight, if you turn away from the ordinary definitions of "the world, the flesh, and the devil," and endeavour shortly to characterize the method of their assaults, you will, I am sure, say, "What I feel in my daily life, is, that I have to contend with *pride and passion*. If I number up all my foes, as they practically present themselves, *these* are the enemies that come most upon me; these are not so much the *efforts*, as the *corps d'armée* of Satan; these are the forms into which he throws the array of his advancing hosts—pride reinforced by passion. How shall I meet them?" You must meet them, my brothers, by *penitence* and *humility;* and indeed when you recognise that you *have* to meet them, then you have gone a long way towards acting "as a soldier."

I say, "when you recognise that you *have* to meet them"—for I am certain that, in some minds I am addressing myself to, there will remain, lurking behind their first easy acknowledgment of the general truth of my statements, a haunting suspicion, that such exhortations lie too high above the plane of ordinary life, to be practicably applicable in the common struggles of every day. My dear brothers, it has ever been said so. "To fight against pride and passion!"—human hearts have often objected—"is not *that* simply to fight against what is *necessary* in the work of the world?" The man who has "to get on," you will say, "must be a man who will put himself forward; he must do so, too, with something like energy and force of character;" and what is that "putting of himself forward"—"putting himself forward with energy"—but a strict adherence in action, to that course which you condemn (professedly with the sanction of an apostle) as "passion and pride"?

Well, let me say honestly, if you are to be a Christian, you will have to prepare yourself to give up in great measure (*always*, if needed, to be *ready* to give up) what the world calls "getting on." If by "getting on," you mean acquiring that which is to be obtained only by the practice of chicanery, pretence, dishonesty —if you mean the advancement at all costs of what is called self-interest, if you mean unscrupulous effort to gain the means of enjoying yourself, not in the lowest pleasures, perhaps, but in such pleasures as the world patronizes, from their adaptability to the cravings of the lower nature; you will have to expect many a check. And yet notice this, energy is one thing, enthusiasm is one thing, pride and passion are quite another. Doubtless, self-conceit, self-assertion "have *their* reward;" doubtless, there is a result appropriate to every course of action; and self-interest in a lower sense, may indeed be served by that which is antagonistic, or at any rate perilous, to the maintenance of real self-respect; for many think that an intimate acquaintance with sin is indispensable to manliness. If in this sense any young man finds that "getting on" implies that he must, as it is called, "see life" (*i.e.* be an adept in the practice of sin) in order to be able to "hold his own;" then, I grant you, that he must abandon such advancement, if he act as a Christian, that he must agree to be defeated, as the world calls defeat, if he is to "endure" hardness "as a soldier." But also, let us not forget this, that the fight against pride and passion, does not imply that in the world you must play the fool; that Christianity places no premium upon laziness, that it does not demand of you to go out of your ordinary occupation. You have to do your duty in the place you are called to, but therein God's claim upon you is not to be forgotten, it is to be remembered *sincerely*. There are men who strive to make, as it is said, "the best of both worlds." *This* sort of respect for God's claim is worse than folly; for indeed there is a fallacy in the phrase; it only means, making the best of this world with a wearying, hollow pretence, of fitfully remembering the other; such men are shut out from the character of the "soldier." But these, after all, are playing at a farce of the most ghastly kind. Better to serve God *or* Baal than to halt betwixt two opinions. Oh, recollect that the world, by its unwilling homage to virtue and high principle, tells these men itself, if they listen to its truer testimony, that they are exceedingly foolish; remember also, that Christian humility does not forbid Christian activity; that you are required to do the duty of your station; that you are required to be earnest and diligent in your common life; that you must be honest to the masters who employ you; honest to the interests demanded of you by the ordinary claims of the work in which God has placed you; but that, amidst it all, the one check and stay to self-advancement to which you must cheerfully submit, is, when it comes to clash with God's demands. For pride and passion must be conquered. Christianity does indeed, in a sense, demand that you shall give up much—very much—which the world will allow you, but it is a false imputation upon the general character of Christianity—an imputation as old as the days of Origen and Tertullian—an imputation repeated again, by some of the leaders of Infidel thought in the last century—it is, I insist, a false accusation against Christianity, to assert that, in fighting as a Christian soldier, you are required to forget the real, the earnest—may I add, the splendid—activities which find or may find their field of exercise in commercial or political life. Oh, no; it is in these very arenas you have to fight. God placed you there; do your duty in them; but oh! not for Time, but for Eternity.

Dear friends, I would remind you, in closing,—if to act with "hardness" "as a good soldier" you are to exercise these virtues, and to keep constantly before you the ever-recurring need of determinedly crushing pride and passion, to be ready to sacrifice every worldly interest that comes in collision with such a demand,—I would remind you of the consoling truth, that, severe as this need of self-denial may be, still the course of the Christian soldier leads to all that is highest and noblest, as the course of the recreant and the coward, who recoils or who turns aside from the battle, leads to all that is basest and worst. For, remember what that is to which Satan is leading you, and his powerful auxiliaries the *world* and the *flesh*.

Sin is a disintegrating force. Sin is a powerful solvent. Sin separates; Virtue unites. Satan leads you to a yawning chasm of discouragement; God leads you to a peak of encouragement, whence you may plainly catch a glimpse of the towering summit of complete achievement. That encouragement from God is twofold. First, with regard to Himself; secondly, with regard to others. For Himself, He has entered the arena of battle. By creation, He willed that the possibility of defeat was, after all, not a counterpoise to the prospect of victory, sufficient to forbid the existence of the world. That is a mystery that you and I cannot altogether fathom. Around the work of our Creator there are robes of darkness, but we know at least this, that God, Who knoweth all, saw that it was better that man should have the possibility of moral ruin, than that he should not have the possibility of spiritual success. Thereby, in creation, God entered the arena of battle. God is with you, my brothers, as you fight. He entered it more distinctly in incarnation; when our blessed Redeemer took our flesh, He did it, to wage the war, not as God simply, but as man, equipped with our nature, fully furnished with our passions, our desires, our hopes, our fears; with the purest of life's joys that belong to us, and I need hardly say the prospect of the darkest sorrows. That great Conqueror lived and struggled under the conditions of our humanity, and when we fight our battle, we are fighting with Jesus at our side.

This week[1] I remind you of a further point in the encouragement that God gives. He entered the arena of battle in the Passion. The great tragedy in the hall of Pilate and the palace of Herod, the great tragedy in the streets of Jerusalem and on the hill of Calvary was not only a tragedy : it was a battle. It was *the* battle at its height; it was the fight of the Captain, Who led the forlorn-hope. Forlorn-hope! It may appear so to men.

[1] This sermon was preached on the Thursday in Passion Week.

Oh, you and I have the great encouragement that when we turn to look at our Master as our Captain, when we enter the arena of contest, God in creation, God in incarnation, God above all in the passion of His sorrow, is fighting side by side with us all. We can "endure hardness as good soldiers," because we are the soldiers of Jesus Christ. That is the encouragement.

But, further, this encouragement is brought home to you by those who are your companions-in-arms.

A distinguished writer of our own day—Mr. Max Müller—struck with the thought, which had written itself in the minds, and in some instances expressed itself in the words, of early Christian teachers—has said something of this sort, that it was by Christianity that the word *barbarian* was erased from the dictionary of mankind, and replaced by *brother*—that in vain, too, we search the pages of Plato and Aristotle for the word *humanity*—that the idea of mankind as one family, the idea of men of all nations becoming children of God, is of purely Christian growth. It is a true testimony, that, before our Redeemer came, men fell into castes and classes, rulers and slaves, Greeks and barbarians; but Christ changed it all.

In this pulpit it has been my privilege, my joy, to recognise the fact at different times, and to call you "brothers" in Christ; in no conventional phrase, but as a real fact, to remember that by one wide law of humanity, by one deeper, more sacred law of redemption, we are bound together heart to heart. And when we come to look at the Christian battle, the encouragement is not merely—although that, we know, is supreme—that God has entered the arena as our companion, but that we are also supporting one another, that we Christians are fighting side by side; that one great power of the soldier, is the encouragement of a brotherhood created by Christ, and that *He* has taught us in our battle to call one another brothers-in-arms. I remember an anecdote told by an officer of the English army, of an occurrence the night before the storming of the Redan, which showed how great an encouragement that sense of brotherhood, so strong amongst soldiers, had been to the heart of one whose courage was flagging in prospect of the next day's terrible slaughter, and how it had helped to bear an inexperienced boy through the trying hours of waiting and anticipation, so terrible to the bravest of men on the eve of a battle. Revelation and experience witness to us all, that in the struggle against the powers of darkness and the forces of sin, *that* strength is not wanting to the Christian soldier.

Have you known a man who is fighting for Jesus, as father, as brother, or as son, in Christ? Your heart leaps up to meet him, and it gives you courage yourself for the battle. Sin is disintegrating; Satan and his forces lead to hatred; hatred is a separation of man from man, and man from God; hatred is the power of murder; hatred is the first-born Evil; that hatred, if it could, would destroy your Creator. The battle of the soldier of Christ is in love. Love strengthens faith. Love is the nerve of life. To love one another and to love God, is the earnest of victory.

O my brothers, when the world is against you; when the flesh, in its awful power, is upon you; when Satan is whispering his subtle allurements; look to the great Captain, look to the incarnate Redeemer; look to Him and see in His face what is written: "Behold the glorious story, My child—I *love* you;" and the love that is poured from the heart of Jesus, *through* the heart of His creatures, is that final encouragement of the soldier in his battle, whereby we are enabled to go forth in the Christian life as a life of struggle, and to "endure hardness" as good soldiers of Jesus Christ. Time is short, Eternity is coming, the battle is thickening; you and I must take our sides.

> "Why with pipe and tabour
> Fool away the light,
> When He bids you labour,
> When He tells you fight?"

SERMON V.

Christian Suffering.

"For it became Him, for Whom are all things, and by Whom are all things, in bringing many sons unto glory, to make the Captain of their salvation perfect through sufferings."—HEBREWS ii. 10.

"PERFECT through sufferings." These words are a statement of a law of Christianity. Throughout the whole of this Epistle, such references to "law" are not infrequent. Continually, as you read the Epistle to the Hebrews, you are struck with such phrases as: "It was necessary, therefore," "it became Him, therefore," "for so it was ordained," and so on, —each of them being simply the initial formula, meant to introduce some law of God's working for and with men. And this, in the text, is that law of the Christian life which comes before us in natural sequence, after those which we have already considered.

Now, if this be the law, let me ask you this question, "What is it that we mean by '*law*'?" When we speak of the world of nature outside ourselves, we mean by "*law*," the regular recurrence of cause and consequence, or—if I may borrow a phrase not my own—

we intend the "observed uniformities in the occurrence of phenomena" which are brought before us in the workings of Nature. Ordinarily speaking, that is what we mean by "*law*." In fact, if we catalogue the effects that we observe from time to time in the outer world, and state them accurately, we are stating "*law*." Need I say that, when we do so, we simply state, as a Christian believes, an expression of *the will of God?*

Now,—not to pause upon this question,—let me ask you further, whether in so analyzing, in so defining, "*law*" it is possible that this may be true of the moral and spiritual world, as well as of the natural? Are there in the moral and spiritual world, in fact, as in the natural world, great and steadfast laws of God? I think I am not too bold, if I answer that certainly there are. Doubtless, these laws are much more mysterious; doubtless, it requires finer faculties of perception, it requires greater powers of harmonizing, to bring them together, as well as to read them, before they are brought together. Doubtless, they are difficult to decipher, difficult to catalogue. They sweep away into the dark distance, so far that many arcs of that circle are lost to the eyes of the watcher, who gazes from Time into the dimness of Eternity. But whether you and I can catch the uniform workings of God, in the spiritual and moral life of men, thoroughly or not, none the less such workings there are; and just as (if a Christian wishes to express *his* way of putting the laws of God, as he looks at Nature) he says, as I have said to you, "*the will of God;*" so also if he wishes more accurately to express God's laws in moral and spiritual life, he says *the expression of the necessities of the nature of God.*

Well, now, if that be at all true, what about the law of the text? Stated shortly, it is this: that *Christian perfection does* (to speak with moderation) in some degree consist in, or *rise out of, Christian suffering.*

Now before we analyze our law, let me ask you whether there is any truth in this Christian description of God's moral and spiritual laws, as *the expression of the necessities of the life of God.* Is there any truth in it, for instance, when applied to such a law as the law of the text? *Christian perfection is a consequence of Christian suffering.* Has that anything to do at all with the necessities of the life of God? The life of God! O my brothers, when you look up unto the "High and Holy One that inhabiteth eternity," when you gaze up towards the Undying Creator, one thing at least you will emphatically answer me: "God by His nature is impassible. He cannot suffer. How dare you, in speaking of God, say that the law of suffering is an expression of the necessities of His nature? If one thing is certain beyond all things, about that majestic Being, it is, that He lies outside the sufferings of our mortal life." Pardon me; all *that* is true, and yet I think the law of the text is an expression also of the necessities of the life of God. For after all, when you look at

God's workings, what is it that you see? If you leave on one side the assumptions, which owe their existence to the critical spirit of materialistic atheism, if, putting all these aside, you look at such mysteries as Creation (not to say Redemption), you will agree with the whole of the Christian Church, that the motive lying behind them must be a motive of love. Now the central core of love is sacrifice; and sacrifice, if it be applied to human life (under the conditions in which human life is known now), sacrifice means suffering; and therefore, if in God there be a spirit of love, in God there is, as is expressed in Creation, as is expressed also in other mysteries, the spirit of sacrifice; that spirit, I repeat, which, when it is brought down to your life and mine in the present conditions of our existence, simply means suffering. So the truth remains impregnable after all, that this very law, if law it be, of the Christian life is *an expression of the necessity of the life of God*.

Now, to turn to the law itself. The law, as I have said, is, that *Christian perfection is a consequence*—at least (speaking moderately) *to a great extent* a consequence—of Christian suffering. Dear friends, if you ask me what is Christian perfection, without going off into a digression on so large a subject, I may say that Christian perfection is the working out of Christian character, up to the height of the Divine ideal. Now it would be certainly a waste of our time to try to imagine, or speculate, how the working out of Christian character would have been, if sin had not entered into the world. That the character of man would have been educated—must have been educated—had sin not entered, is an incontrovertible truth. God, when He created other things, "saw" that they were very "good." God, when He created man, did not speak specially of him with that finality, for God intended man to grow, and stretch forth his powers, up to a higher perfection; and, even if sin had never entered this poor pain-stricken world, there still would have been a need of an advance towards perfection, by some exercise of the law of sacrifice.

But, without pretending to speculate upon what would have been, turn to what *is*. As a matter of fact sin *has* entered: as a matter of fact Christian character *has* to go on towards perfection.

Now, the means by which Christian character is to go on to that perfection, is Christian suffering; for, in order that you may have perfection, in order that your Christian character may be crowned, it must be consolidated by the acquirement of Christian virtues; and it is by the power of suffering, that Christian virtues are acquired. We cannot travel through the whole catalogue of those distinctive virtues which mark the Christian's life, but we can take one or two, and see if our law applies. Let me take examples from three. Well, first of all, I affirm that Christian *humility*, which is one of the very deepest, most fundamental, as well as most beautiful, of Christian virtues, is the result of Christian suffering. My friends, I have said it in this pulpit more than once—it is a fact that cannot be gainsaid—that humility is a creation of Christianity. The ancient world never dreamt of humility; had you talked to it of being humble, it would have considered you a fool; but the moment that Christianity came into the world there came the fresh thought—humility. And Christian suffering does this —it makes a man see himself in his own actual being; not through the distorted medium of his vain conceits and fancies, but driving him down into the inner seat of actual life, compels him to see what he *is*—a mere atom in God's creation; and to *realize* that you are a mere atom in God's creation, to realize this under the eye of God—*that* is humility. So, the virtue of humility is necessary to Christian perfection, and the virtue of humility may be produced through suffering.

It is quite as true to say, although at first sight it seems paradoxical, that patience—for which I prayed this afternoon in the Collect[1] of the Church for this week —is also a creation of Christianity. Now here, perhaps, some may be inclined to join issue with me. You may be inclined to assert, if you have read any of the stories of the ancient world, that ancient thinkers understood

[1] The Collect for the Sunday next before Easter.

patience. If you look more carefully, however, you will, I think, agree with me, that they did not. Ancient thinkers, even the best of them,—even the Stoic philosophers with whom St. Paul had to argue,—mistook not merely the character (though they recognised the being) of a God, but they mistook the ordinary virtue of patience. There was in them, it is truly asserted, a kind of earnest and determined resistance to the terrible facts of life; a kind of "defiance of destiny." There was a kind of dogged stubbornness taught; there was a kind of hopeless, joyless, submission to the inevitable trials of our mortal existence; nay, there was something *like* resignation, but it was only the resignation of man, not for the sake of God or himself, but for the sake of some ideal conception of the universe, insisted upon by the old thinkers of the time. It remained for the new revelation of the Prophet of Nazareth, to bring home to the thoughts of man, the virtue of patience.

All virtues, after all, are only varieties of Divine Love in the soul. You call them by different names, but they are only divine love, looked at in its action, in different ways. The other day I reminded you that patience was love in the effort of resistance. It is so, indeed. Divine charity, in one of its forms, is the virtue of patience; and until divine charity came into the world, that virtue, as the Christian understands it, could not possibly be brought forth. That it was brought forth, that it ruled, is a fact of Christian history from the moment of the crucifixion of Jesus. From the moment of that supreme exhibition of patience, the virtue shone out upon the world. You know how continually the apostles insist upon it. You know how we are taught that the "trial of our faith" is to "work *patience*." You know how our blessed Lord Himself, speaking out of the mystery of His glory, speaking through the mouth of the blessed John, urges upon the Bishop of the Church of Laodicea, that he shall buy of Him "gold tried in the fire." *That,* holy men have believed to be simply Christian love, tried in the fire of affliction, and coming out in the virtue of patience. And you remember that in the same way, the Apostle John himself—when he is trying to sum up the power of victory, as he saw it in that other world in his revelation, at Patmos—can find no better expression for that conquest of the Beast, wrought through suffering, than these words: "Here is the *patience* and the faith of the saints." Patience—Christian patience—goes to make Christian perfection; and if humility *may* be, patience *must* be, a result of suffering.

I instance one virtue more. We all of us, if we consider humility by the power of the natural man—if we look at patience simply as intelligent beings, trying to analyze it, without thinking spiritually of what it means—we all of us, are apt to look upon both, as passive virtues. But, at least, *courage* is not passive. Courage is demanded in the Christian life.

If we are to rise near to Christian perfection—once more this afternoon I insist upon the fact—we have need of courage. You know it every day you live. You know it in every station of life that you occupy. You and I want courage to speak the truth in ordinary social life, courage to throw ourselves against the affectations of society, courage to declare God's counsel, in the face of a world that more than half denies Him; you need courage to go into your warehouses and act honestly, courage to sit in your drawing-rooms and conduct yourselves not as society demands in its unreality, but as God insists; courage to speak out for God in life, courage to meet the dead and vacant stare, courage to confront the sneer of ridicule, courage to support you against the cold, hard pressure of a heavy and unbelieving world. If you are to have Christian perfection, you must not play the dastard when you go forth to the battle for God, and therefore supremely you are in need of courage.

Now courage is born of suffering. Courage is a victory over the affection of fear. Courage is the outcome of an inner strength. Courage, even philosophers tell us, demands considerable cultivation, and the chief power of cultivation, the chief power of discipline, given by Christianity, is the *suffering* revealed on the Cross. If you and I are to crown our Christian life with courage, it must be by Christian suffering. "Perfect through suffering." Thus, then, if you are to go on to Christian perfection, there is the one way. I might apply it to other Christian virtues: I have given you a sufficient sample, by applying it to three.

Well, if it be so, we may readily see how it is that the whole life of the Christian, by acting upon this principle, at once elevated and purified. Without going any further into an analysis of virtues, let me speak broadly of facts in our Christian experience. You and I, if we are to go on to perfection, require elevation of nature, and purification of heart. What are *the* powers of purification and elevation? I answer, without the slightest fear of challenge, the power of separation, and the power of aspiration towards God; or, to put it in simpler language, the *power of sacrifice* and the *power of prayer*.

Now prayer pre-eminently springs from suffering. If a man prays, he lives. If you say your prayers in a morning, your soul has about it a strength for the day. If hurry, or laziness, or stress of business, or slothfulness, having prevented you from rising at the hour at which you intended to rise, has kept you from saying your prayers; if you content yourself with some feeble substitute, by repeating words to God, as you move about your bedroom, dressing for the day, instead of kneeling down and saying the prayers that you owe to your God as a duty; if you satisfy yourself when rushing down to business, by just salving your conscience over, with a stray thought of devotion, or a psalm or hymn or collect repeated;—recollect that (because you are, in a *perfunctory* manner, doing that which ought to be done in a *careful* manner, and as the first of duties) you are throwing your mind and your conscience, your heart and your life, open to the most seductive attractions of pleasure, and the most deadly stains of sin. The man that prays, lives. The soul that prays, can never be lost. Prayer is *elevation* of our life; prayer is the ennobling of character; prayer is the ascension of the soul, into the presence-chamber of the Eternal Monarch; prayer is the prostration of the soul in that presence-chamber, to receive the benediction of the King. You need prayer, if indeed you need life. How are you to learn it? My friends, the early Christians, who knew how to pray in a sense that most of us, perhaps, have long forgotten or never known, learned it through suffering. "Is any afflicted," says the apostle, not (in our modern fashion) "let him complain against God;" no, but "let him pray;" and when the Divine John, in another vision like that to which I have just referred you, gazed into the very heart of the mysteries of the blessed dead, he saw the souls of the martyrs crying from beneath the throne, and the cry that they uttered was only a continued expression of a long-established habit—having prayed on earth, they prayed in heaven. They learned to pray through suffering.

Ah! you and I may think lightly of prayers when we are taking "a sunny view" of life, when our pulse beats quick, when our brains are clear, when our health is strong, when our circumstances are satisfactory. We may then, indeed, put aside from us much of the thought of the necessity and the blessing of prayer. But, once let the clouds come, once let us lose a friend whom we have loved, once let us stand face to face with the great revealer—Death; once let health give way, or circumstances change, or sorrows rain down upon us with a deadly deluge, then, *then* pre-eminently, if we are Christians, we learn to pray. The power of elevation is prayer, and prayer in its deepest sense is learned through suffering. "Perfect through suffering."

And if that be the power of elevation, what is the power of purification? Purification comes, you know—I am speaking generally—from a deep sense of immortality. To measure trifles at their full value, to put things in their true places, to see things not as they *seem* but as they *are*—*that* is like perspective applied to a picture, like proportion applied to a building; it is to throw back what has been putting itself forward too prominently, to draw forward what, for the moment, seemed too much in the background, to reduce to harmony what once was confusion. Now life—mortal life—once an elevation of trifles with the depression of what is important—is painted in that perspective, reduced to that harmony, brought to that proportion, by the deepening sense of immortality. It is that which makes us feel, every moment, that we were formed for better things than simply to trifle life away, as if it were a dream. Now that sense of immortality is deepened through suffering; for it is suffering that teaches us what this world *is*, in its real sense—how hollow its professions, how changing its opinions, how fawning its applause, how worthless all it gives, compared to the high satisfaction of that which comes out of an immortal creature's immortal life.

It is suffering that brings the gayest, the most trifling to be real at last. Therefore it is suffering that helps to purify our lives. You will remember—if you look back to the history of that great convulsion which shook Europe to its centre in the latter part of the last, and early part of the present, century—you will remember, among the most prominent victims of the French Revolution one striking and attractive figure. The Queen of France, in the early days of her reign, certainly led a life that, if innocent, was sufficiently trifling. Whether or not it was the dulness, and chilling nature of Louis XVI. that drove Marie Antoinette to wile away the weary hours of royalty, in the harmless pastimes of the Palace of the Trianon, hers, at least, were employments scarcely worthy of a queen; but as you look upon the several acts of that terrible drama, first of all the frightful anxieties in the first outburst at Versailles—then the horrors on the 20th of June, as the king and queen faced the mob in their palace in Paris—

and finally, the ghastly days, whose closing hours were black with the gloom of the Conciergerie—all of them, you feel, step by step, process by process, combined to change that young, light, trifling girl into the majestic figure of most noble womanhood, that looks out to us from the scaffold in the Place de la Révolution, with sad eyes, and face marked with suffering. She had learned the sense of immortality,—to stand above the trifles of life,—because God had visited her heart with a sharp and terrible scourge of suffering.

It has always been so with Christians. To feel the sense of immortality, to rise out of the trifles of a day, to touch to the quick the life that we are leading, needs, to some extent, suffering.

"Perfect through suffering." I have been careful to say that Christian perfection comes from *Christian* suffering. Suffering in itself works no perfection. The first action of suffering is to turn the soul in upon itself, and if the soul be not trying to learn of Christ, then it becomes, in a more deadly degree, intensely selfish. It is an old thought of Christian theology that there are two great centres of the life of souls in this world—the one is, self, the other is, God. To be conscious of self intensely is the part of a sinner; to be conscious of God intensely is the perfection of a saint; to be passing from the one consciousness to the other is to be advancing in the Christian life. Now, suffering is a force that either drives the life all the more intensely into self, or more intensely on to God. There are conditions in the exercise of suffering upon the fulfilment of which depends its power to lead from self to God. Of those conditions I will mention two.

(1) If your suffering is Christian suffering, it must be *willingly accepted for the love of God*. Merely to suffer is not at all to be a Christian; but to suffer with a voluntary acceptance for the love of God, is to infuse into suffering a power of eternity, that comes from the Cross of Christ. (2) To suffer as a Christian is not only *that*; it implies also *looking unto Him*; to keep our eyes steadily fixed upon the King of suffering, is to see what suffering was, in God's *life*, as He came to bear sin in His human nature. "Looking unto Jesus, the Author and Finisher of our faith,"—to do *that*, as well as willingly to accept such trials and sorrows as life brings —*that* is, to suffer as a Christian, and *that* is to go on unto perfection.

These are conditions for Christian suffering. Next, what results may we hope for from them? You may say, "Suffering is a high thing. This world I live in is fairly comfortable; my circumstances are easy; my life is calm. Am I to throw myself into unreal duties? Am I to look right and left to see if I can find something or other keen and sharp?" Certainly not. Suffering in a high degree, *is* a high thing. Suffering in its highest degree, is very often the talent that God keeps for those dear ones who have most closely followed the Lamb—for those elect souls who have been obedient to the light from first to last. But you and I, O my brother, my sister—you and I, in our low-lying common life—you and I, with our disobedience to conscience—you and I, with our carelessness about truth—you and I, with our indifference to duty—you and I, with our impure hearts, our thoughtless lives, our forsaking of God's ruling for us, from the first dawn of reason till now—you and I, may hardly be fit subjects for the great trials of the martyrs; and yet we can scarcely escape *some* trial—we may touch, *must* in some sense be touched by, that sacred thing. You cannot pass through life without *some* suffering.

Well then, shall your suffering be the fire that withers your life, that leaves it in ashes, that makes it a mere crumbling ruin? Or shall it be a power which shall raise you up to the life of your Creator, make you walk with the steady step of princes, and prepare you for the perfection of the glory of God? That is a question for life. And the answer depends, you know, upon those conditions which I have enumerated. Will you take it *willingly, for the love of God*, and as you take it, will you *look unto Jesus*, "the Author and Finisher of your faith"? Men have done it, weak women have done it. History is full of records of it. Stephen died with a face like an angel, praying for his murderers—"perfect through suffering." Paul the aged marched to his death with a stately step and quiet smile; and I am certain that when that hoary head, separated from the body, rolled in the dust of the Ostian Way, the lips were firmly set, and that old face was calm and smiling, because he had accepted the law of his being—"perfect through suffering." Men and women have done it in more modern times. History of later ages, tells us of a mother who clasped her baby in her arms amidst the flames, and spent her time thanking God that He had delivered the child, who was suffering with her, from denying the Crucified One. We, in our own day, all remember the thrilling spectacle of a murdered prelate of God's Church dying with right hand raised, and white lips parted in the act of benediction; and, in more recent years, we know how in our own part of the Church, one of our bishops,[1] the great missionary bishop who went out to work in one of our distant dependencies, died at his post a martyr's death, with unflinching courage and calm resolution—"perfect through suffering."

Men and women have done it—why not you and I? He may not call us to marvellous martyrdom; He may not call us to high places in His kingdom; but to each of us He gives some trying hour; to each of us He gives the fret, the worry, the weariness, the sorrow that comes inevitably to every immortal life in the bonds of Time, and *that* is a touch of true suffering, if we mark it with the Cross. Accept

[1] Bishop Pattison.

it then. My message to you now is a definite one. We are in the Holy Week. We have reached the time which all the Christian Churches in every age have recognised as the most solemn of the year. We are coming step by step nearer to those bleeding feet, and looking up to God's law of sacrifice worked out in the incarnate life—worked out in the tragedy of the Passion, of our Divine Redeemer. Are we going, not only to seek Him as our atoning Sacrifice, but also to follow Him as the great "Captain of our salvation"? We must follow as He leads. His life is a life of mystery, but He is the one Mediator; He took our humanity, in one way different from us indeed, for we have it by identity—that human nature—and He by union; in another way different indeed, for His everlasting beatitude never failed or fainted, whilst yet at the same moment He was deluged in sorrow. But that perfect humanity, and that perfect deity, while they necessitated such miracles in His person, enabled the reproduction of miracles analogous to them, in the persons of each one of us by our union with Him.

To be "one with Christ" is to have an everlasting beatitude. To be "one with Christ" is to partake of His endless joy; but if we are to partake of that, if we are to have that beatitude, it must be on the same conditions, and by the same means—"perfect through suffering."

To conclude: philosophers profess to submit every

asserted law of nature to the test of verification. We Christians need not shrink from following their example. A verification of the law before us is supplied by the great crucifix on Calvary. Christ crucified is the verification of that law. Do you want to see a *man?* Then don't go to him who haunts the scenes of pleasure. Don't go to the sensualist, who says he is "seeing life" when he is obeying his passions. Don't go to a great teacher, who can philosophically explain, but can never act. Go to Calvary; look at that lacerated form; look at those bleeding wounds; look at the face of Jesus our Redeemer. The law that sweeps throughout God's creation is verified. He, *the* Man, the one Man worth the imitating, worth the thinking of, worth the following—" the Captain of our salvation "— verified the law of God, for He was "perfect through suffering." And, oh how perfect! Not one flaw, not one failure, not one break in that magnificent perfection. If you want to try your law scientifically, verify it at the Cross of your Redeemer. Having proved the law, how can you use it? How can *your own* suffering be of real value? The answer is this. Suffering is a hard thing; it is a hard and a cruel thing, until it comes under the Cross of Christ; but *then* it is of fresh power, although it is of deeper intensity—and why?

There is one beautiful name in Scripture, a name which goes to every heart that is in sorrow. The Agent Who applies to our lives the life and work of our

Redeemer, is called by a name that meets our sorrows: He is called *the Comforter*. The Spirit of God *applies* the life of Jesus. His work is to take that life and show it to your necessity, to impress it upon your heart, to unite it to your being; and as He does so, He requires, it may be, that sharp, sharp wounds shall be inflicted upon you, according to the sufferings of Jesus, but He touches and heals them with tender breath as *the Comforter*. Sin-laden souls, immortal creatures born for glory—oh, remember, pleasure, mere pleasure, will first hide, and then dwarf, and then kill, all that is high within you; but that if all you do—whether it be amusement, whether it be pleasure, whether it be duty in life—be marked with the Cross of Christ, then all that—right in itself, good in itself—is raised to a higher power, is made, not only a passing influence, but a real and a lasting energy; for everything that has force to lead you onward in life is made "perfect through suffering."

Accept your law; live for God; go to Jesus; follow that great example; look at that splendid picture; and then indeed you will long, more and more, that each sin may be erased and effaced from your character; you will long, more and more, for that spotless holiness which you and I cannot have here, but which, in its degree, grows in us by the power of Jesus brought to us by the Comforter, till we near the grave. And if there be one stain, one blot, one remnant left upon the soul, forgiven, indeed, but darkened by upbraiding memory, when we pass into eternity, then, at least, we shall have the power of *that* suffering which comes from the first sight of One that we have loved, ah! far too little, that we have known in His beauty, ah! not so as we ought to have known Him; but Whom, as we meet Him, pained to think how much we misunderstood Him, we shall joy to find, in His glory, powerful to cleanse; we shall rejoice by the very pain and the sweetness of the vision, to be fitted to gaze on and to love Him for ever—" perfect through suffering."

You are born for perfection if you are born for glory. There is one path, as there is one end. That end is the crown given to those who triumph. That path is the path of sorrows by the Cross of Jesus Christ.

Dear friends, I pause. I have kept you too long, but it is difficult to close when one approaches the great tragedy, with its unfathomable depths of meaning; I add only this word. One of the greatest poets of the world has told us—translated into a well-known phrase by a poet of our own—that the " sorrow's crown of sorrow is remembering happier things." So it is in the ordinary workings of the world. Dante speaks truth here as always. To remember happiness that is gone, is the sharp " crown of sorrow;" but when Jesus touches you with the magic influence of the Blood of His majestic Passion, then the " crown of sorrow " ceases to be a mere memory, or a bitter regret; it becomes the splendour of a real repentance, adorned with the final glory which awaits the redeemed at the feet of our Redeemer, when we kneel, weary, travel-soiled, but in safety, before the throne of God.

SERMON VI.

Christian Joy.

"Who for the joy that was set before Him endured the Cross, despising the shame, and is set down at the right hand of the throne of God."
—HEBREWS xii. 2.

WE have endeavoured, dear friends, together, throughout this Lent, to sketch certain features—certain characteristic features—of the Christian life; and it must be confessed that, as we have tried to sketch them line by line, under the action of our pencil, that life has stood out, to speak honestly, severe. The neophyte may well say, as he looks at it, that such a life is like to scare one, if his desire is to act in it as in anything else he undertakes, with thoroughness, earnestness, and determination. It may be so; but, whether it is likely to scare us or not, I cannot agree to retract one word of what I have said. The Christian life is a life of labour; it is a life of struggling advance; a life of constant watching; a life of energetic battle; a life that must look forward year after year for more and more suffering, to lead it on to the path of perfection. But, even though all that be true, yet there is nothing about it to daunt the energies of the really earnest man.

CHRISTIAN JOY

I come, to-day, with some thoughts which may at least help to soften the hard lines of the picture. And yet indeed if we would bear in mind, that fundamental principle which lies behind the Christian life, those lines would appear, thereby, softened. The great principle of the Christian life, is the principle of faith.

Faith *implies* all that I have said; it implies work and labour. There is a supposed contrariety, in some minds, between faith and works; but faith is a principle that implies practice. If there be faith, there must be toil. Faith teaches us that there is a responsibility to an unseen Being. Faith lifts us off the platform of common life on to the level of a higher world. Faith, therefore, if it does—and it certainly does—imply toil and struggle, at the same time implies great, and constantly increasing compensation. To consider the principle of faith would alone soften the picture; but the text, my final text this Lent, contributes much more to that softening. The text reveals to us a world of mystery, because it reveals to us a world of motive.

Well now, recollect that you never enter upon anything more mysterious than when you enter upon the region of *motive*. The words of the apostle here act like the angel of the Apocalypse who opened for the blessed John a door in heaven: *these* words open for us a door in eternity—they reveal to us *a mystery of motive.* You and I are very often perplexed in ourselves by that mystery. Nothing is so confusing as to contemplate motive. If we go deeply into our motives, we are staggered at once. There appears so much that may be good; there is certainly so much that is bad; there is such a complex network of cause and effect; there is so much mixture and intermixture of what seems to belong to God, and what assuredly springs from self, that when we examine our motives, we are not infrequently sorely perplexed; timid natures are hopelessly staggered by the thought of their motives. Some natures indeed "refuse to be comforted:" they are not content with honest prayerful earnestness in keeping motive pure, with sincere and fitting self-search to discover and bewail unworthiness of motive that vitiates worthiness of act; having done what they could, they waste force in fruitless fretting that they cannot do more; they tease themselves by a habit of chronic debating whether or not they are *certain* of purity of motive. Sometimes (I do not speak from mere fancy; I speak from practical experience) it is asked, "How am I to *know* that my motives are good?" It may be a fair question, sometimes of course it is, when meant to elicit advice as to the best method of that strict judgment of self, which is the duty of all of us; but very often it expects no answer, and will be content with none; it is the result of the morbid posture of a mind inclined too much to fall back upon itself. And to fall back upon one's self in this way, is a mark of a nature in a condition of deplorable weakness, a nature that forgets trust in God, a nature that loses sight of His greatness and His goodness, a nature that is wanting in distinctness of purpose, a nature, above all, that does not recognise the supplementary power of the infinite merits of our Redeemer. It is very right, it is very needful to examine ourselves on our motives, but it is an unhappy expenditure of strength, to torture one's soul by demanding *certainty*, in a subject-matter where certainty is unattainable. We must do our utmost to be true, and when all is done, our pure motives will still probably be soiled with some alloy of evil. The thought should make us humble; it need not lead to morbid failure. There is nothing gained by scrupulosity. Nevertheless the very failure, the very scrupulosity of such a nature implies a *mystery of motive*.

Well, then, if this text speaks of motive, it opens to us a world of mystery; and it does not open it merely to show us that it *is* mysterious, but to make the mystery plain. For, O my brothers, when we want to read something of motive, where can we read it better than in that great chart which maps out for us the intricacies of this mortal life, in the chart of the mind of Jesus our Redeemer? The text does nothing less than this: it reveals to us, to speak with carefulness, at least *a* motive in the life of Jesus; and that motive, oh! think of it, if you have agreed with me that the Christian life is a severe life—the motive of Jesus was joy: "For *the joy* that was set before Him He endured the Cross."

Well, then, I ask what was the cause of the Saviour's

joy? I do not pretend to give an exhaustive answer. Of course it would be an assumption of knowledge about that Divine character, that no man dare to pretend to; but at least you and I may humbly and reverently believe that three causes lay behind the joy of the crucified Redeemer.

First of all, there was *the joy of redemption*. We cannot pause to enter upon that mystery, but at least notice this: the greatest painter—at least one of the greatest painters—of the devoutest period of the middle age, a man who, as men said, used to kneel and pray till the angels came to him to be painted, whose works, as they adorn the walls of Florence, open up to us a world we had hardly dreamt of before,—that greatest of painters—Fra Angelico da Fiesole—in some of his most beautiful pictures, has, amidst a multitude of exquisitely-pencilled faces combined in groups, made *each* face of varying expression, but *each* expressive gaze of joy and thankfulness steadily fixed upon one central figure—the figure of the Redeemer. And the Redeemer, while not apparently gazing directly at any one of them, yet with an expression of exceeding joy, raises His hands in benediction over all. It is only a figure of a real fact, a fact that our Redeemer—the Head of Creation—recognises,—cannot be happy except as recognising. It is only an artistic statement of the truth that to raise up all our natures to the realization of His own central life (that we may accept Him as the centre of all we do), to lift up these natures into their true dignity, or (to put it in plain language) to forgive and cleanse our sins, and then to draw us up to that life of divine worship, for which we are born, is nothing else than the joy of Jesus for which He "endured the Cross and despised the shame." *It was the joy of redemption.*

I pass on. It was more: *it was the joy of union.*

Surely there is nothing so sad in life, as the sadness of partings. I listened the other day to two little children talk—two little simple children—without any experience of the sorrows of life. They were about to part for a short time, and I overheard their words. "I am so sorry to leave you, dear," said one, almost an infant. "And so am I, so sorry to part with *you.*" What was the meaning of such words from young lips? Dear innocent hearts! They knew little or nothing of the sorrows of life. For them all *that* was to come; if black the future, the present was in sunlight. My friends, it was the expression of one of those deep truths which lie buried in the very essence of our mortal nature. It was the expression of the pang of parting. Partings are the saddest things in life. Partings create sorrows whilst we are living; partings robe the beds of death in the deepest gloom; partings fill the eyes of the dying with looks of anguish; partings make our hearts ache as we gaze at those who lie before us loved and dead.

What, then, is the greatest joy of life? The joy, I

answer, of union—to be united with those we love never to part. It is not the joy simply of the creature. Oh! blessed be God, it is the joy of our Redeemer. The cause of that joy—you have anticipated it—the cause of the joy which carried Him along the path of sorrows, which bore Him over the dangers and sufferings of the Cross—was the sense that He had set out upon His march to a complete union, not with God, not with angels, not with high intelligences, but, O my sinful brothers, with *you*. It was the sense that He would be united with you and me—*that* was the joy of Jesus Christ—united to part no more. *There was the secret of His mysterious motive.*

I must touch on one other secret to make the motive plain: the joy of our Redeemer was not only, then, for redemption and union—it was joy supremely *for the glory of God.*

The glory of God! May I repeat myself for a moment this afternoon in summing up what I have said—may I repeat to you in substance something of what I said some weeks ago during the Manchester mission, and ask you to think again what it is we mean by "glory"? We mean, as it seems to me, at all times essentially the same thing, although it expresses itself under very different conditions. In nature, you have certain things glorious. You look out, over a stretch of country, and see it clothed in the beauties of early summer. If any of you have been in Southern Italy when the spring is bursting forth in all her splendour, you have seen the dazzling spectacle of long reaches of land simply robed and decorated, nay, bathed and saturated with flowers; when you gaze upon such a spectacle as that, you exclaim involuntarily, "It is glorious!" Or here, in our own beautiful green England, when you get out of the city smoke, the noise, and the toil, and the confusion of your daily life; when you go away to rest yourself in country places amidst our northern hills, and look on the summer evening, as it spreads itself in its splendour over the summer sea; when you watch the setting of the sun, that washes the waves in purple, or crimson, or gold, your very heart leaps up within you, and you call this "a glorious scene." And, when you turn to the life of man, the same sort of thought will force itself upon you. You look at a splendid character; you see him environed with difficulties; you contemplate him as he marches through those difficulties with a steady step, with a fixed determination, with the earnest exertion, and the sustained effort, which belongs to every noble and well-strung nature; you look at him perhaps across long chasms of ages, perhaps in dim glimpses down long vistas of history, perhaps next door to you in some ordinary common friend; and yet when you see such splendid characteristics marking that life you are constrained to say, "It is glorious." You have sometimes imagined a man, as being indeed one, but he has fallen beneath the dignity of his being, he has become a sensualist, intemperate, careless, and, wherever you yourself have stood on the moral platform of life, your first impulse (a wrong, but a natural one) has been to despise that man. You checked that impulse—weak yourself, you learned, if a Christian, to be sad, not contemptuous, at another's fall. But why that impulse? Because once see a man rise to higher things, and you know that for *every* soul there is a possibility of aim and achievement, better than all the lower nature can supply. You have realized the high result of grace, seeking to clothe it in words you call it "glory."

Now, "the glory of God" is the source of all glory. The glory of God bursts forth, as fire from the life of God. The glory of God is manifested in many ways. Sometimes, when we look at Creation, we call it power; sometimes, when we look at revelation, we call it truth; sometimes,—ah! thank God more often—when we rise up in our weakness, and stretch forth our arms through darkness to clasp some one who will feel for us an everlasting affection, we call it by the splendid, the subduing name of love. But, whatever name you call it by, you at least recognise this, that God Himself, in the sum total of His majestic attributes, wherever and however He expresses Himself, expresses Himself in *glory*. What did the Redeemer long for? He longed that the angels might read the mysteries of His own everlasting life. He longed that His creatures might rise up, out of the lower levels of their short probation, into the higher region, where they could gaze at the life of God. He longed—to put it in a common but pregnant phrase—He longed for *the glory of God.* That was His joy. It was the passion of His life; it bore Him through the desolation of His death.

Well, if it be so, what is the *power*—to look more closely at it—what is the *power* of joy? Such as it was in Jesus, such will it be in us. He is the Head of our humanity. What was the power? I answer, it was the power of exaltation. It was like that sense of immortality of which I spoke to you last Tuesday, it was a power that raised. Nature tells you so. You go out on a bright spring morning into the green fields, you hear above you a voice that thrills you through with pleasure; you don't see anything distinctly; but from the clouds there comes a warbling note, a rising splendour of music, as the lark ascends towards heaven. There is in every cadence the outwelling of an unconscious, yet real, joy. It is a parable of God's working. The little creature, as she ascends and sings, sings and ascends, is simply proclaiming the truth that was seen in the life of Jesus: joy is a *power to exalt.*

It is more than a power of exaltation. It is a *principle of expansion.* Such thoughts as these are too wide to touch only for a moment, and yet I *touch* them and that is all. What you and I want is expansion. St. Paul, in his own language, some of you will remember, calls one of the gifts of the Spirit—*broad-mindedness* (our Bibles, in their English, are incorrect in the translation)—a large-mindedness, a heart that expands into open reaches, that is not smothered with trifles, but can take in a great question in its entirety. What is one of the sorrows and the degradations of life? Why, that we are so narrow-minded, that we take narrow views of one another's thoughts, put narrow constructions upon one another's deeds, that we do not take a broad view of the great questions of human life. Now joy is an expansive power—the joy of God. Just because it is "of God," because it is a part out of that great broad life of our Creator, it expands the heart of the creature. Was there ever a heart so big as the great heart of Jesus? That heart opened out to, and embraced, the whole family of poor weak mankind.

Further, it is a *principle of strength*. It upholds; it prevents us falling down into the mire and clay, into the darkness and sadness of sorrow. Joy raises us above the world, for it opens out what some men would call an imaginary, but what I dare to call a real, though a spiritual, world. The joy of God tears asunder the clouds; it opens the doors of heaven; if it springs up in any heart it makes that heart strong to breast the trials of circumstance, because circumstance is only a passing thing, and eternal life *is* eternal.

If you are to be strong in your Christian life, that life must be crowned with this last benediction. It must be a life not only of labour, of advance, of watching, of battle, of suffering—it must be a *life of joy.* Is it so? I turn from the Lord our Redeemer, I turn for a moment to ourselves, and I answer;—" In a real sense, it is, or it ought to be." "As He was, so are we in this world." As the Head of humanity, so the members of the great family, if they be united with that Head. Our life may be a life of joy: is it like His joy? Yes, in part, yet not altogether; for in part, as becomes a creature, there is a difference of condition; and as there is a difference of condition, there will be a variation of expression of the joy in us, which is, however, the same essentially as the joy in Him.

Why may I give you joy? Why may I have joy? Because we are immortal. If we were mortal, then indeed there would be sorrow. The positivist philosophy, which has invaded the regions of modern thought, and is haunting the imaginations of this generation—haunting especially those who give their life to thought; haunting indistinctly those whose lives are impregnated with the thoughts of others, although they are themselves immersed in labour—the positivist philosophy, amongst others of its gospels, teaches us that life ends with the grave; that all we have to look for, is what they call a *subjective immortality,* which amounts to the shadowy conception, that those who are left behind us, will remember us, for a time at least, when we are gone. I give them a present of their conception, and I wish them joy of it, although so far as there is any good in it, it is not very new. But I think I may say in my own name and yours, that if we are earnest men, we are above such vagaries and such fancies, that to imagine that you and I, in life, can console ourselves with the hope of a mere *subjective immortality*, is to imagine that we are dreamers or fools. I think we meet few *dreamers* in Manchester; however men may dream who give themselves over to speculative thought in seats of learning, at least in this great city of energetic toil, I am not in danger of meeting with the disciples of a dream.

What you and I want, my brother, is a deepening sense of immortality—that we are immortal. To feel that there is life within us, is, whatever men may say, to feel that there is joy.

" 'Tis life, whereof our nerves are scant,
Oh life, not death, for which we pant;
More life, and fuller, that we want."

It is life that gives us joy. The sense of life is blessedness. It has been said, and said in a most exquisite argument, carefully elaborated by a modern writer, whose book has been in the hands of many of us not many months ago,—it has been said in that striking volume of sermons published by Professor Mozley, before the hand of sickness struck him with its paralyzing stroke, it is said, in a phrase pregnant with truth, that to deny immortality is to be guilty of an "apostasy from reason;" and it is so, because, for a man to say that his life ends—is not to contradict external evidence, it is to contradict one of the first facts of internal consciousness. Now to *feel* this fact keenly, to *feel* that we are immortal, once to realize the fact, is to raise us out of a low-lying life, to place us in the midst of eternal splendours, and to stand in the midst of those eternal splendours is, I submit, to have joy. *I joy because I am immortal.*

I joy because my Christian life implies also a *completeness of final union*—final union with all that is holy and beautiful and good. If we have to struggle in life, the struggle sometimes is hard. If we have to watch perpetually, watching sometimes is difficult. But if we know that one day most certainly—as certainly as that we, this afternoon, are assembled together in this Cathedral—the bonds that bind us to the Head of our humanity shall be so tightened that they never can again be broken; that there can be no more temptation, no more sin, no more low ways, no more base thoughts, no more miserable aims, no more mixed motives; if we feel that we shall be eternally one with Him and He with us,—all these trials sit lightly upon us; the hope of that completeness of union is joy.

For these reasons we have a right to rejoice; if we are Christians we are one with Christ; the union will be completed in eternity. And, there is further reason for our joy—a reason not despicable in a life of labour: we joy because there is coming—"there remaineth," as the Scripture beautifully says, "a rest." To the best of us life is toil. With all the happiness that God may give us in His goodness, with all the dear friends, kind thoughts, loving sympathies, sweet affections, pleasant circumstances—everything that can make life brightest—life at its best, is full of labour, full of weariness; and the more we advance in it, the more conscious we become of this fact. My friends, there is "the rest that remaineth"—"remaineth for the people of God." See here a distinction between the worldling and the Christian in their thoughts of rest—the worldling tries to find his rest *now;* the Christian is content that it should be *then;* but if he looks on to that rest, and knows that it is coming, oh, what are the few years of labour! oh, what the struggles of battle! there is a source of joy in that full, that fruitful thought: "There remaineth a rest for the people of God."

"As He was, so are we in this world"—we have causes which produce *that* in us which moved Him. The power then that moved Him may be fruitful in ourselves; we may be moved along the same path of suffering by the same, the magnificent motive, that was at work in the soul of Jesus—the motive of joy. The Christian life is a life of joy. Oh, indeed it is. Doubtless there are clouds of darkness. Doubtless there are difficulties around us. In the physical world there is the mystery of pain. In the intellectual world there is the difficulty of ignorance. In the moral world there is the sadness of sin. But, after all, what are these? They are only the dark clouds that throw out the sunlight; they are only a sombre background (like the backgrounds of Salvator Rosa) that brings out the splendours of the picture, carefully drawn by the pencil of the Holy Ghost the Comforter. Sin, if there be sin, implies that there is such a thing as sanctity; sorrow, if there be sorrow, implies that there is such a thing as satisfaction. Sin is an invader. Sin is not the rightful possessor of this house of our humanity. We have opened the door to him, we have admitted him, and having admitted him we must fight him; but oh, the true guest, for you and me, as Christians, the true guest is joy. Ah, whatever darkness there is in life, the Christian life is a life of joy.

It is so for all these reasons.

May I remind you that there is one reason more. It is a life of joy *because of the abundance of grace.* You may be distressed when I dwell on the fact of so much labour, toil, struggle, battle; but oh, these difficulties, if they are faced, dwindle into nothing, when you think of the grace of God. "I came," said Jesus our Redeemer, "that they might have life, and that they might have it *more abundantly.*" He came that grace might be abundant; and so it is. As the dews in the morning, in the warm summer, so are the actual graces of God that penetrate day by day the longing, thirsting soul. They are hidden; we cannot see them; but we know that they *are*, and if they are hidden they are only like Nature. There are spots in the world that are most beautiful—morning by morning, night by night—though you and I, in the murky atmosphere of Manchester, and in the toil of our life, may never gaze upon them. There are quiet valleys, long stretches of sea, open expanses of heaven, myriads of twinkling stars, dazzling splendours of worlds of ice,—glories which, as they stretch away unseen, unpeopled, in God's vast creation, seem to be wasted; but the angels are gazing at them, and they are but a parable of grace. Grace is hidden, but grace is real. It is God's life, God's strength, God's beauty, God's love, applied to man to help him towards the Divine ideal. Once make trial of that help so lavishly offered, and you may joy in the joy of your Creator. "As the mountains stand about Jerusalem, so standeth the Lord God round about His people."

Will you then be altogether mournful? Gloom is a part of a diseased sensibility. Gloom belongs to a morbid nature. There is no *gloom* for the Christian. No, he has fixed his eye on one object. He has set his purpose to one end. The object is the glory of God; the end is the attainment of everlasting union. He is gazing at no abstract idea. He does not stop at a mere imagination. It is all thrown into concrete form; the shapeless mass is hewn into an actual, a living, statue. That statue is the person of a once sorrowing, now glorified Christ. The Christian life is a personal attachment. If you are to answer the question, "Why have I joy?" or, "Why am I to struggle?"—if you are to explain the *rationale* of "watching," it all comes to this, "He loved *me*, and gave Himself for *me*." Oh, it is a glorious thing to say, "I love Jesus;" but facts are better than feelings; it is a grander thing to say, "Jesus loves me." That is the joy of our life; that is the underlying spring of our purification; that it is that carries us on in the midst of sorrow, and from that, in sorrow, we have joy. Doubt comes and darkens us; sadness comes and spreads its gloomy mantle over us; penitence comes and makes tears flow; but, in them all, there is that wonderful spring of activity, for in them all, to a Christian, there is the touch of the love of our Redeemer. "Love," some one says, "if it be moral, implies obedience, and obedience, if it be unfettered, implies love;" and both, when they come together, and are expressed in our work for Jesus, throw out from them a power which carries us on to eternity, and that is the power of joy: "For the *joy* that was set before Him He endured the Cross, despising the shame."

Well, my brothers, there is one practical thought that I ought to give you before I close, and I divide it into two parts. It is this: You have a *duty* if you are a Christian. Converted Christian, your duty is the duty of cheerfulness and thanksgiving. A gloomy Christianity may be a particular phase or variety of Puritanism, but it is not a part of that beautiful life, which is the life of the Gospel of Christ. You have a duty to fight against your gloom, a duty to be thankful to God. Life is rich in blessings. Ah, even those who have been plunged in the darkest sorrows have felt it; poets have taught us how minds in the blackness and the gloom of struggle, yet have realized that Nature herself, coming as God's messenger, speaks to us of joy.

> "I wondered at the bounteous hours,
> The slow result of winter showers:
> You scarce could see the grass for flowers.
>
> I wondered, while I paced along:
> The woods were filled so full with song,
> There seemed no room for sense of wrong.
>
> So variously seemed all things wrought,
> I marvelled how the mind was brought
> To anchor, by one gloomy thought." [1]

That is one thought; and another is this. To-day is a solemn day. To-day—the Thursday in Holy Week—is Maundy Thursday. What is Maundy Thursday? What is the meaning of that strange name? It means a day of a *great command*. The great command, first of all, in spiritual matters; then in practical fact. The great spiritual command— that we are to love God and love one another. "If ye love Me keep My *commandments.*" "If ye are My disciples love one another." "A new commandment give I unto you, that ye have love one to another," —and love means joy. The great command also in

[1] Tennyson's "Two Voices."

practical fact; it is the day of the institution of the Blessed Sacrament—the day of that Sacrament of loving union which unites us with Jesus.

Are you preparing for Easter Communion? Are you going in penitence to your Redeemer? Are you determined that the bright morning of the Resurrection shall see you, for once at least, obeying that unchanging command: "This do in remembrance of Me"? To be a Christian is to love Jesus. To love Jesus is to obey His commands; and that Christian who wilfully slights the sacrament of union—that closest "point of contact" —as it has been called—with the incarnate Person of our Redeemer—that Christian cannot be said, if he knows what he is doing, to be a Christian at all. These are two plain duties that come out of the motive of joy, for joy springs from love.

Here, then, I have done. I have spoken to you this Lent, as God has permitted me, of some few Characteristics of the Christian life. The Christian life, my friends, is a life of mystery; "it is a life hidden with Christ in God." It is involved in darkness. Men cannot read it. You and I cannot thoroughly understand it. But it is more than a life of mystery. It is a life of beauty; it is like the glories and splendours of the bright spring mornings. It is like the colours of the southern mountains when they are bathed in the brightness of the rising dawn. It is like the sweetness of a calm evening that speaks indeed of a dark night coming, but reminds us, that beyond the night, there is a morn of glory. The Christian life is a scene of chequered shade and sunshine. "A little sun, a little rain, and then night sweeps across the plain, and all things fade away." The Christian life looks steadily at death, but it looks beyond death to immortality. The Christian life looks to immortality, but it looks through immortality to an infinity of glory. The Christian life through that glory, penetrates still further,—and there, at the very apex of creation, *there*, in the very fire of God, the eye never rests until it rests at last, as it shall rest eternally, upon One Who has loved the soul that is gazing upon Him, One to Whom the soul is to be united, and in Whom it shall find its satisfaction for ever, when it "sees Him as He is."

My friends, remember again—for I repeat myself—that I am trying to imprint one thought upon your memories, namely, that to hold all truth, to do all duty, to exercise all faculties, to reason to the utmost, to remember the revelation of God, is nothing, it makes the whole life other than Christian, unless your life be a life, in some sense, of *personal devotion;* and personal devotion is the energetic exercise of will, and thought, and affection, upon that one magnificent vision which shines upon us at this time above all, and is ever shining—the vision of the Eternal manifest in the flesh, manifest in sorrow,—Jesus of Nazareth, our King, our Redeemer, and our God.

Personal devotion is the very soul of the Christian life.

I charge you to pray that *you* may have it. I beseech you to live by it. To-morrow comes with its message of sorrow. Look across Good Friday, for the moment, and you see the dawn of the Resurrection; but, oh, that you may go to your Easter with joy, *keep* your Good Friday. Keep the Good Friday of this life of sorrow, and in the midst of its darkness, its gloom, and its trial, you will have the upspringing joy of the Resurrection, which is the joy of the presence of Jesus our Lord. Divine Redeemer, most loved, most lovable presence, ever near us, never forsaking us, always bearing with us, still beckoning us on, hear us and help. O hard heart, O failing life, if you have forgotten the One Who is noblest, best, most loving, go to Jesus, and *tell* Him you have forgotten Him. "I came," saith He, "to your weak and failing nature." "I came 'to seek and to save that which was lost,' and if you seek Me here, the joy will merge into the eternal ecstasy—everlasting union."

> "Jesus, Master, King of Glory,
>   Still to Thee we turn for life;
> Master, when the battle's sorest,
>   Oh, sustain us in the strife.
>
> So when all at last is over,
>   And we rest with Thee above,
> We shall swell Thy heart's rejoicing
>   With the rapture of our love."

SERMON VII.[1]

For the Love of Man.

"Bear ye one another's burdens, and so fulfil the law of Christ."—
GALATIANS vi. 2.

THE Galatian Epistle, as most of you will remember, was directed, at least in one main stream of its argument, against that phase of reactionary Judaism which St. Paul so dreaded as a barrier against the spread of the Gospel of Christ. And the writer, in dealing with this dangerous obstruction, not only takes for granted throughout, but also names, that strong, subtle, free, supernatural force, which every Christian preacher must at least *understand*, if he name it not,—the force by which alone all truth can be applied to the soul—that force which we designate, and rightly, the Grace of God.

But then it is to be remembered that this "grace of God" falls, so to speak, in the soul of the Christian, into certain permanent forms. That is, that the application of Divine Grace is through special impulse; and to turn

---

[1] This, and the two following Sermons on the Motives of the Christian Life, were preached in Manchester Cathedral at the midday service on some week-days in Advent 1877.

to this special impulse, and these permanent forms, brings us face to face with the mystery of Christian motive. Of this I now speak. I shall not attempt to dive into the depths of Divine Grace, or to estimate or analyze either its measure or its meaning; but only to examine it in some of its resultant impulses, in some of its permanent forms. I mean, in fact, to invite you to contemplate *some motives of the Christian life*.

Now it is true that I once ventured from this place to warn you against an over-scrupulous habit of scrutiny in the region of motive.[1] I do not, however, contradict myself now. For I believe that it is a clear view of higher motives, which at once reveals and defeats our meaner impulses; which assists the discipline of *proper* self-searching, by making it healthy and hopeful; and resists any habit of morbid introspectiveness with its fatal tendency to paralyze activity of character.

Well then, first of all, the statement of the text may be regarded as indicating one *aspect* of the sovereign Christian motive. And throughout we have to deal not so much with three motives as with three *aspects* of one. I begin, then, with that which lies more distinctly on the surface, and which is, therefore, far from being the deepest of all, but which none the less is inextricably connected with all below.

In dwelling upon the motive of the text, we cannot of course put altogether out of mind the living source

[1]. "Characteristics," Christian Joy, pp. 119-121.

from which it springs. But although we do not ignore the person and vitality of the Lawgiver, we are concerned to-day simply and strictly with obedience to the law. The motive of the text, then, is this—the desire of unqualified obedience to what is called "the law of Christ." This law in plain words is the law of "my duty to my neighbour,"—as the Catechism puts it in familiar phrase,—the law, called "of Christ" because promulgated and sanctioned by His authority; the law binding upon all reasonable creatures, the law of *the love of man as man*.

Such, then, is my contention, that grace operating in the heart of the Christian, will assume at least—and for the present I content myself with saying "at least"—*this* permanent form,—the recognition of "my duty to my neighbour,"—the real and energetic "*love of man as man*."

Now, first of all, let us remember that this motive was wholly new. Of it the Greek and Roman philosophers knew absolutely nothing. Reason, the human Reason, in those debased forms of it which were the only forms attained by the very highest examples of heathen thought, was the one and only rule by which the philosophers of Rome and Greece attempted to regulate conduct. They had forgotten, altogether forgotten, at least in any practically efficient sense, the presence and the influence of God as a regulating check on the Reason of man. And when Paul stood, on a memorable occasion, denouncing the idolatry of the great Greek city, upon the Areopagus; when Paul stood amidst the magic splendours of Grecian art, beneath the azure canopy of an Athenian sky, and recalled His hearers to the thought of the one God, Whom in their ignorance they faintly remembered, but scarcely worshipped; he *startled* them by his promise of so clear a revelation, but the shock of his electric word was intensified by the continued vibrations of the thought which followed it; God, he said, "hath made *of one blood all nations of men.*" It was not merely the thought of a manifested God that struck them, not merely even the startling statement of the Resurrection miracle (though *that* was the climax of the apostle's proclamation) which astounded them; but through both they had to face a fresh, a bewildering revelation: viz. that God's government and the creature's destiny implied a new, an undreamt-of motive—the love of man as man.

And then again, let us not forget that if the motive was new to the world—it was not only new in extent, and new in manner of presentation, it was new essentially in what I may call its very texture; and that, therefore, —paradoxical as the statement may appear,—because thus new, it is as potent now as then.

Selfishness, you will agree with me, is the adamantine barrier which stands in the way of duty. It is by our innate selfishness that we are turned aside from that path; but conscience witnesses distinctly still what is the true direction of our life.

Only a few months ago it happened to me to watch the surging swell of the waves of the Mediterranean as they rolled landward under stress of a sudden storm at sea; I watched them dash against the opposing barrier of a breakwater on the seaboard of Africa. The waves seemed almost living things, with such steady rush, with such unwearying persistence, did they return again and again to the charge; but as the storm rose, and they were borne with increasing violence against the granite blocks, the sea-swell—stayed by the obstructing masses—turned aside and swept round by the narrow entrance into the harbour within. Though checked in its course by the barrier, it rushed at last to its resting-place, by changing its channel. But there had been storms on that coast—we saw their traces—in which, amid the screaming of the frenzied wind, and the hollow booming of the resounding sea, the mass of maddened waters had risen against that barrier, and upheaved and tumbled the huge blocks of granite in wild confusion, as if they had been mere tiny pebbles tossed by an infant's hand.

Now so it is in human life. Put up the barrier of selfishness, yet stimulate men's strength by what is called "the moral sentiment"—then it is certainly true that a far-sighted man, possessing the force of self-regard, may succeed by that force, not indeed in breaking down his opposing selfishness, but in reaching to something like a fulfilment of duty. But, my friends—discarding metaphors—if all barriers are to be swept away, if no selfish cravings are to restrain a man from reaching towards the height to which his conscience points, if he is seriously to recognise, earnestly to act upon, the "infinite claims of duty," a mere self-regarding principle won't do, he needs a power dominating his *entire* being; energetic, and therefore—for man is a deathless spirit—supernatural; he needs the force of a motive, quickened by the inspiring breath of the living God—a motive strong to smash through, fierce to sweep away, all barriers of opposing selfishness—and such a motive is *the love of man as man.*

The motive was new, but it supplied a needed force, and therefore it is lasting.

My friends, let us ask ourselves a further question: Is the law by which this motive is brought home to man indeed Divine? I answer that it is, that Christendom is right, that the ancient world was wrong; for this rests upon truths which haunt the chambers of the thoughts of mankind, most truly human, therefore most really Divine. For I submit that any great and true teacher, if he is to apply any force to the Christian life, must rest that force upon a real *basis of thought.* It is impossible for you and me, if we are in deadly earnest, to stand upon mere moonshine in the struggles of this mortal life. And our Blessed Lord, and His apostles after Him, were in real and deadly earnest when they taught man the mystery of motive. And so it was that they were not wanting in care to lay a foundation of thought; for they knew (to borrow in part another's thought) that man's best affections, strongest currents of will and desire, cannot fail to be influenced by, as in turn they influence, his deepest and most sincere convictions. And so Jesus and His followers, teaching this motive, have never been wanting in suggestion of fundamental thought.

There are, then, three chief principal thoughts which form a basis of this motive of the Christian life.

First, in strict conformity with the general teaching of our Blessed Redeemer, and His apostles after Him, we may base it upon a recognition of *the dignity of man*, his dignity in all departments of his being, body and soul. In his soul, Christ called our attention to the truth, that he is an emanation from, a spark of, Divinity. Pardon me, my brother, if I change the third person rather into the second, and say that you yourself are such; that there is a real dignity about your soul; first, because you are the antecedent thought; then the realized conception; finally the fully equipped and gifted creature of God; first playing as "a thing of beauty" on the mind—if I may so say—of the Eternal; then coming forth shaped by the hand of that Divine Sculptor, stepping into the world as His thought, a thought of His creative genius, finding its permanent expression in your personal, individual life. Such is the dignity of the soul; and Jesus taught it, when He asked, What would it profit if the whole wide universe of external nature were grasped in the hand of a living creature, and he had failed to possess himself of that which is *the* handiwork of his God, which is, therefore, of lasting consequence —his own immortal soul? "What shall it profit a man if he gain the whole world, and lose his own soul? or what shall a man give in exchange for his soul?"

I need hardly add that if the Lord laid such a foundation for such a motive, in teaching the dignity of the soul, He did not, to say the least of it, forget *the dignity of the body*. He reminded men again and again, if by nothing else, certainly by the activity of His Divine compassion (and His apostles following Him did the same), that the body, as it now shares man's corruption, so shall it share man's glory. He taught men *that* at which sceptics sneer; *that* at which "modern thought" is confounded; He taught, as the truth, *that* which you and I are therefore bound to believe, not the permanence of particles of matter,—of that Christ and the creeds of Christendom say not one syllable,—but He taught that the fact of the identity of the body (of which, while every material particle in it changes, we still are cognizant from infancy to mature manhood and later life) is a fact which maintains its enduring significance, not only to the close of our lifetime in this world, but in unbroken sequence beyond the grave. He taught you that the body, with its limitation of senses, shares the wound of ignorance of the soul; but that this partner of our mortality is to be a partner for ever, for that, though divorced at the moment of death, there will be a reunion in heavenly nuptials; a reunion when the weakness is ended and the wound is healed, that "He shall change the body of our humiliation, that it may be fashioned like unto the body of His glory." He taught you—and St. Paul draws forth the result of that thought, of that teaching—that you, like your fellows, are dignified in soul *and body*—therefore the motive "for love of man as man."

There was a second foundation in thought which the Lord laid during His life. He taught the possibility —do not start at such a thought—the possibility of our perfection. Teachers of philosophy in our own day have claimed to give us a good deal of light about "the perfectibility of man." Christianity is no whit behind the thought of philosophers in teaching so magnificent a lesson. But Christianity does not dwell solely upon the perfectibility of *the Race*, much less upon intellectual development as the practical process. Christianity reminds us that perfection is relative; that though you and I may not rise to the highest conceivable perfection, we may, we *must*, endeavour to rise to that degree of perfection which God has intended to be ours, and to which He has called us by His inner voice and His providential guidance through external circumstances.

You, my brother, you, my sister, have a perfection of

your own,—to fill your own place in life;—to learn that lesson of your own education which God intends for you; to have your own affections purified, your own will braced, your own mind developed, your own being elevated to the highest point which it is possible for *you* to attain. That is *your* perfection. Keep the lofty idea of your Father before you, as your Lord commanded, try to struggle up to it; use the means He has provided; and, if "in Christ," then indeed you shall ultimately reach the goal. This second principle of truth upon which such a motive may securely stand is the perfectibility of man. Can you be careless of one endowed with such a capacity? hence the motive —*for the love of man as man.*

And I will add a third and last foundation; it is this. It is what I may call *the pathos of a common destiny.* That all men were "made of one blood" was the cry of the apostle on the heights of Areopagus, a proclamation involving surely the pathos of a common destiny. Jesus knew and emphasized the truth not only by His teaching, but in His own sacred person.

Need I remind you how He did so? how He accentuated it by the throbbings of His own tender heart?

The common *destiny of service,* for instance, belongs to us all, be we where we may—in the ranks of thinkers, or the ranks of toilers; in the ranks of those who have to use the brain for others, or those who have to present the fruits of thought, embodied in the work of the hand; be we where we may, we have a common destiny—a destiny of service, accentuated, intensified by our dear Lord's own assertion—" I am amongst you as He that serveth."

Again, we have a common *destiny of death.* All of us have a share—think of it for a moment, —a thing so common that we are apt to forget it, but so certain that we are bound to remember—all of us have a share in a common destiny of death. Our poor hearts

> " Like muffled drums are beating
> Funeral marches to the grave."

Whether you be a peer of the realm, or a wealthy merchant of Manchester—still face the trite but solemn truth—when you are side by side with the poor debased beggar in the streets of your city, you are standing by one to whom you are bound by the tie of a common destiny—subjects alike of the awful, the tragic, the pathetic certainty which I call the destiny of death.

And again, we are bound together by the common *destiny of a splendid immortality.* That which is within you lives and shall live. It is only the germ of a life which may unfold itself in beauty. Every affection that is washed in the Blood of Jesus, and vivified by the energy of grace; every power of thought within you, which is surrendered to that Primal Thought Who is above you and beyond, and yet within you too, each of these may live, and live for ever in the completeness of perfect glory. You and I are bound together by the destiny of immortality. And *at least* upon these three foundations—for I do not pretend to exhaust in them the thoughts of our Master—at least upon these three foundations there is based that moving motive—strong enough to supply us with energy, diligence, and directness in the path of human struggle—the motive of whose power the earthly life of Jesus was the most exquisite expression—*the love of man as man*. Surely these foundations are incontestably solid and supporting. Were it otherwise it would be difficult indeed to act under so Divine an impulse.

Human life as it presents itself in its common concrete forms is often, alas! in the deepest degree repulsive; but the meanest, the most degraded examples of our race have still in them some lingering lineaments of their heavenly Prototype. To be keen-sighted to the blurs on our own bespattered characters, because the eye is habituated to that exquisite ideal, because we have "seen white Presences upon the hills," and " heard the voices of the eternal Gods," is an inevitable consequence of persevering faithfulness, *and* it is to learn humility. I do not dwell upon that at present. But I do insist on this, that it is a part of the same temper to pierce beneath the outer coverings of human sinfulness, and see the real, though ruined, beauty of human souls.

To dwell upon a common destiny is to learn leniency to faults in others, which—with our richer opportunities—deserve *in us* severity, and which we recognise as only (it may be exaggerations of) our own. To meditate on the dignity of humanity is to fix the attention on an inner and real excellence; for Nature, being God's work, is beautiful, even amidst corruption and decay. And to recognise a possibility of better things is to fan the smouldering embers of a human pity, and a dreamy admiration, into the devouring furnace-flames of Christian love.

Nor is there anything vague, or shadowy, or unsubstantial in such a motive. St. Paul gives no encouragement to a dream of labouring for *the Race*, except so far as we labour for each component of it, for, in fact, the *individual man*.

The first glow of love may shine out from the thought of an ideal, an abstraction, but only when we see its object in our actual friend, or brother, neighbour, dependant, child; only when we tear to shreds the wrappings of conventional selfishness, and see the value of an individual soul, *only then* is it warm, is it living: "Bear ye *one another's* burdens, and so fulfil the law of Christ."

If it be so, my brothers, let us then state precisely what the motive is. I have said what it is based upon, and I have named it in a manner. Let me name it nakedly. Yes, I will name it, for its name rings in the heart of Jesus; a name before which even benevolence pales, for benevolence may be of cultivated kindliness, this is of supernatural grace. Let us contemplate its splendour, for up there in heaven, and down here on earth, it is the same in its exquisite characteristics, though different in degree. It is that which "suffereth long and is kind," "thinketh not the evil," "beareth all things," "never faileth." It is Divine charity; it is Christian love.

What is love? Love is the march of the soul out of all that is selfish in self into the life and the interests of another. Love is the power by which the being passes out of the shades of night and enters into the chambers of the morning. Love is the strength by which our own inner self-conscious principle emerges from the subterranean chambers of the dead and enters into the temples of the Undying. What are those temples? Are they the majestic productions of mediæval genius, with pointed arches, fretted roofs, and decorated capitals? Are they the fanes which Gothic architects have reared for the admiration of future generations? Not so. The young, the aged—you in the prime of life, you in the declining day—*you* are the temples of the living God; and the heart of the Christian, when he loves as Christ loves, passes from his own subterranean chambers of selfish anxieties and deathly care, and enters into the living chambers of desolated human hearts. Love is the forgetfulness of self in the thought for the interests of another. Christian love for our fellows is the passage of life from its own narrow darkened precincts, journeying through the heart of Jesus the Redeemer, and centreing in the heart of man. Such is the motive of a Christian—*the love of man as man.*

The aged apostle, who listened to the heart-throbs of the Redeemer, startled Ephesus, and startled Asia I doubt not, when he taught his own favourite lesson —"Love one another." The aged apostle, who had once denied his Master, and was won back at the sight of that face of uncreated loveliness, startled the great Babylon of the nations, you may be sure, when he wrote in his apostolic letter, "See that ye love one another, with a pure heart, fervently." The aged apostle who died on the Ostian Way not far from the gates of Rome, St. Paul—our teacher in the text —astounded his correspondent, I am certain, as he melts us now to tenderness, when he besought a slavemaster at Colosse to take back his runaway slave, " now," he said, "as a brother beloved specially to me, but how much more unto thee."

Such was the new motive with which Christianity awakened the world. My brethren, does it only startle you now, or does it come home? Does it not sound with the real ring of that voice of God which echoes through conscience, and finds its answering whisper in your inmost hearts? Remember that it is a great reality; that it is learned in its fullest significance when the soul has a hearty desire to obey the law of the Lawgiver. This is one part, at least, of the truth, of which, amid the misty cross paths of thought and tradition, we may be unquestioningly secure—that if we are to be Christians in some measure, and follow Jesus Christ, we *must* learn "the love of man as man." Out of it comes an atmosphere of compassion; out of it comes the purification of friendship; out of it comes the energy of intercessory prayer. On *this* point I pause. It is a question requiring unabated repetition, Are you praying for others? I ask it, and I beseech you drive the question home. Be sure it is this motive which gives the energy so to do; and surely it is a comfort to your soul, O my Christian brother, when you can do nothing else for a world that is wallowing in wickedness, that you can spend some time by night, or by day, in kneeling at the foot of the Cross of Jesus, and interceding for your brethren; yes, it *is* a comfort, if you love man as man. From such a motive arise compassion and prayer.

And remember; this, like other motives, strengthens with the using. We must try to act unselfishly *as if* men were worth helping, and we soon find they *are*. There are cases indeed that baffle and perplex, there are those about us from whom truth seems to have vanished, to have declined and died from sheer atrophy of neglect.

One of the bitterest lessons of advancing life is the necessity of less trustfulness in intercourse with the world. Ah me! yes, life is a tragedy, a soul's tragedy. In trade, chicanery and cunning pass for cleverness; in society, "gossip and scandal and spite" are clothed in fashionable or conventional language, but though more refined, they are not less malignant than the cruel tittle tattle of lower life. Half the news of the daily papers, in which we find our daily food, can only be collected by "keeping a sharp eye" on the faults of one another; or if faults and *fiascos* are not forthcoming, from the same sources are supplied hints that they may be expected soon. Among religious people, ill-nature and evil surmisings find their way to the very step of the altar, or have their allotted place in the corner of "the roomy pew." Ah! there is nothing more saddening, nothing more startling than the littleness and the greatness of man.

One thing at least we each can do. We can *try* not to add to the evil, but to make a life so dark as this, by one streak brighter, a world so sorrowful, in some slight measure less joyless by our presence in the gloom. It is possible to be sincere yet kind; possible to see the best rather than the worst in human character; possible to make the most of what is good. Some truer recollection of our own grave and depressing faults, amidst, all the time, our conscious sincerity, will often teach a lesson of long-suffering and charity towards our fellow-men. In fact we can *be kind*. The age we live in is one of social perplexity. As years go on that perplexity seems to increase. Our great cities are sinks of iniquity; the relation of master and servant, workman and employé, is out of joint. Waifs and strays, little ragged homeless urchins, with bright faces and merry voices,—for they are still too young to be subdued by sorrow,—are tossed about our city. Beneath the gas-lamps the giant selfishness is plying its devilish trade in "the great sin of great cities." What can we do? Reverse the question and you have the answer, let us *do* what we *can*. Each soul helped is a great work done. Don't add to the sin and sorrow yourself, relieve it when you may.

On the grim St. Gothard, even in the later summer, the snow lies white along the ledges of the mountains, and the clouds, on their jagged crests, sweep murky and chill; the peasant climbs the grassy patches with his heavy burden, grave, toil-worn, determined; when the clouds break and the blue relieves the severity of chilling snow and unrelenting stone, on the scarce yet splendid summer morning, even the life-worn mountaineers find voice for song. In this, our huge black city too, the world seems some handbreadths better when the morning sunlight breaks the fog. An unselfish life is a streak of sweetest sunlight in the sin-tried crowd. At least we can be kind. "Kind words," you will say, "are cheap." I beg your pardon. If truly kind they mean a kind heart, and, in a world so false and irritating, *that* means severe self-discipline and faithful prayer, a stern hand against wrong, a gentle temper to weakness, an abandonment of the ready tendency to sharp and cruel criticism, so easy, so self-pleasing, but so unbecoming in frail and failing creatures such as we. At least *be kind*. The world will be the brighter, your own soul nearer God; a new vision of life in its responsibilities and blessings, will open to the eye; selfishness —the root of all the sorrow—will diminish; increase of strength for fruitful effort, will be given with the increasing habit and effectiveness of the motive, "bearing others' burdens," "love of man as man."

Anything more? Oh, remember this, in your hour of work: it is in *this* motive that there is found the stimulus of that attractive force, by which the young become apostles of Jesus and print the story of His life in the hearts of their fellows;—the force of a Christian example, of a consistent and courageous life, of adherence to principles which are thought over, not only thought over but grasped, not only grasped but loved, not only loved but lived. The force of your example men *must* feel, if Christianity as a living power within you, has fixed such a motive in your inmost heart. Oh, if thus it be, though you may never *speak* a word on religion, believe me, you are preparing the kingdom of God.

I have done. I close with that thought—" preparing

the kingdom of God." That is what Advent means. Christ is coming, coming quickly, though men think He is lingering; to the ear tuned by Divine hope, to the eye keen with Divine faith, to the whole being thrilling with the love of the Saviour, believe me —though it be far away still (as it *may* be) across the ages, or if it be near (as it *may* be) in our own time —there sound the footfalls of the coming Redeemer, and therefore we try to "prepare the kingdom of God." Act from Christian motives and you take your part in preparation.

And indeed there is a call—oh, believe me, you live in an antichristian century, you live where Antichrist exists, for Antichrist (though eventually he may be a person) at first is a temper and a spirit. The temper and the spirit that endeavours to inspire the movements of human life, the temper which arises from mere rationalistic thought, or philosophic teaching, as the evening miasma from the marshes of the Maremma; the temper and the spirit that endeavours to guide the mind, to brace the will, to warm the heart— one could smile, but for sorrow, at the absurdity of it— without the living force of that God, from Whom comes the inspiration of every true thought and noble emotion of our life, that temper, whether it finds its expression in the temples of worship, or in the marts of commercial enterprise, or in the great Houses of the Legislature of England, or in the humble dwelling of the poor; where-ever it is, it is Antichrist; and you and I can best withstand it by positive action, by "preparing the kingdom of God." Do you prepare it, then, at least in this way—by drinking in, recollecting, loving, living by this motive which comes from the King. Do not try to put philanthropy in stead of Christianity; do not try to "bear the burdens" of a mere abstraction—as some systems teach—instead of "the burdens" of living sufferers, of "one another," as the apostle commands from Christ; do not try to kindle affections, without the true basis of faith upon which they must rest, and the true fire of faith from which they must glow. Do not attempt to do the impossible, but fall back upon obedience to a severe but blessed injunction, "Bear ye one another's burdens, and so fulfil the law of Christ." Go out, then, into Manchester and help those who are around you. Go out into Manchester and love those that hate you. Go out into Manchester and let the love within you be felt by those you deal with in the common exigencies of trade. Love, I say. How are you to do it? Only when you recognise the Sovereign, can you catch the spirit of loyalty; only when you respect the Lawgiver, can you recognise the claim of the law. Do not then coldly, thoughtlessly, place rationalistic fancy in the place of the fact of the coming Jesus, do not try to substitute the calculations of utility for the invigorating motive—the desire of obedience to a law which comes from the living God.

Lift up your hearts, my brothers; *Sursum Corda!* Christ is coming! Gaze at *Him*, in His approaching Advent, and say to *Him*, "My Lord, my Master, have I forgotten Thee in my pitiable selfishness? only help me, henceforth I will act upon Thy teaching, bear my brother's burdens, and so fulfil the law of Christ!"

SERMON VIII.[1]

For the sake of Jesus.

"Blessed are ye, when men shall revile you, and persecute you, and shall say all manner of evil against you falsely, for My sake."—
St. Matthew v. 11.

I PROCEED to-day to a deeper, a more strictly supernatural motive in the Christian life.

It is the one which holds a middle place in that trilogy—if so I may phrase it—with which we are now concerned; it may be said, with a certain degree of accuracy, to connect the lower, and yet powerful, motive of which we thought last, with the highest, the grandest, the most comprehensive of all, to which, please God, I shall next direct your attention; it holds a position in the region of ideas, analogous to the office of the Redeemer in the region of fact; it occupies, so to speak, a mediatorial place.

The first eleven verses of the chapter from which the text is taken contain in few words some of the most remarkable among the spiritual revelations made by

---

[1] This sermon was also preached, with some difference of treatment, in St. Mary's Church, Nottingham, on Thursday, October 30, 1879.

Christ; nothing less than an unveiling of the laws on which depends man's true, man's highest happiness, as seen by the unerring wisdom of God.

Now in casting the eye over the "Beatitudes," we cannot fail to notice two striking facts: first, that in the earlier six at least, and in truth (though not so evidently) in the seventh, the idea of happiness presented, connects itself with the inner life, not with outer circumstances; and secondly, that on the contrary, the last—whether in its *general* form in the tenth verse, or in its more *particular* application in the eleventh—*seems*, at any rate, to depend upon outer circumstance, while it certainly assumes the existence of a *special* connection between the soul that is blessed and the Lord Himself.

Is it, then, in reality, *essentially* different from the others? And if not, does this implied connection with the person of the Redeemer explain the apparent anomaly?

Let us pause to answer these questions. Well, then, the Lord Jesus undoubtedly makes *this* idea of happiness connect itself with His own Divine person in a manner which, to say the least, is not apparent in His statement of the others. Notice, then, the manner of this connection. Here occurs a memorable phrase, not found in the other seven; one of those forcible utterances which, century after century, live on in the heart of Christendom; the connecting link in thought: "For My sake."

Before the eyes of the Redeemer, as He sat on the

mount of the beatitudes, there would seem to have arisen in vision the opposing legions of those two mighty armies which still divide the world—the army of Evil and the army of Good. And the words of Jesus, like the touches of a painter, throw out the vision in the form of a powerful picture, in which the eyes of those who will, may see depicted the characters of both. He implies of the legions of Evil—whether deceived or deceiving—that they are apt to be positively opposed to God, energetically cruel, and characteristically false; and He suggests the corresponding fact that the mighty army of opponents, the army of God's Israel, is known by "notes" precisely the reverse. They meet in conflict. And so fierce, so overpowering, so masterful is the onslaught of the Evil that they can but be described as persecutors; so apparently feeble, so helpless, so hidden the resistance of their adversaries, that they can best be called the victims of persecution.

Is it, then, this outer circumstance, is it the mere fact that they *are* persecuted which constitutes the characteristic blessedness of the people of God? Certainly it is not. For indeed there *can* be no special blessedness in the bare fact of being abused, no inherent joy to any being possessed of human sensibilities in being called hard names, and that too, as the Lord's words imply, with vigour and malignity. No; nor does the fact of falsehood in such onslaughts make the victims "blessed." Very often you and I may be subjected to stinging reproaches, may be labelled with titles which are scarcely complimentary; the specific charges may satisfy at least *one* condition in the Lord's description, they may be absolutely, they may be even impudently false; and yet if we know our own hearts, if we habitually scrutinize our own conduct under the light of the Divine Presence, we shall feel that though *this* attack is strikingly unsuitable, still, sinners as we are, it is evident to us, of our own knowledge, that we richly deserve as much or more. The joy, then, is not necessarily consequent upon the being found fault with, nor even upon the being found fault with *falsely*, but it has its root in the existence of *that special connection with Himself*, which irritates the opponents of our Master into a hostile temper, or rouses them to overt acts of persecution; in *that*—to the existence of which such persecution is the clearest testimony—in *that* which is, which can be nothing else than *a supernatural fact of character*.

My friends, a supernatural fact of character implies many inflowings of spiritual power, many and difficult exercises of moral choice, many exhibitions of external energy. And if *this* fact is so real, and so rooted in the being of the soul, that it can successfully bear up against those forces of evil whom its existence excites to hostility, then indeed that soul is the proper subject for Divine congratulation, "Blessed art thou." And thus we see that, like the other beatitudes, this one describes, in truth, a condition—most beautiful, most marvellous —of the inner life.

Oh, indeed the real blessedness of those supplied with this force, perfected in this feature of supernatural beauty, is not that they are attacked, nor that they are *falsely* attacked by the armies of Evil, but that the attacking spirit is roused into activity by encountering a soul, over which a sacred Presence is increasingly asserting its influence, whose course is becoming daily more simple, whose power of sustained endurance daily more steadfast, through the submission of its every energy to the sway of one overmastering motive—the most tender, the most penetrating, the most persuasive —a spring of blessedness, because an evidence of love— the motive of personal devotion to one Master, summed shortly in the heart-stirring condition of solemn beatitude—" For My sake."

Well then, I make no apology for passing from the broader subject of the verse, and fastening your attention on this one point. The motive which is intended to take the central place in the life of a Christian is *the love of Jesus Christ*. That is, if it be true that you and I ought to act, ought to endeavour to act, from *love to man as man*, as Christians we are bound to go farther, to go deeper. We are enabled to possess ourselves of a secret force, by which what might be weak because general, becomes strong because particular, which strengthens and sustains that other motive in a vigorous vitality, and that secret force is a supernatural, yet personal attachment, according to apostolic testimony, love for our Master, or, I repeat, as the Lord Himself phrases it, "For My sake."

Well then, let us analyze and interpret this secret force.

I. And first of all its strength of mastery lies in this, —it is an appeal to the hearts of us all by the power of *a most blessed memory.*

I am sure no societies, no classes of civilized mankind, have in any age been impervious to the touch of such a motive. The old Greeks in their later times of degeneracy and decline, looked back, as to a source of life, to the ancient glories of the days of Pericles; the Jews, when they recollected what they once had been, and in their days of mourning hoped yet again to rise to better things, did not fail to fire one another's courage by the inspiriting recollections of the conquests of Joshua, of the wide-reaching glories of the empire of Solomon, or even of the short-lived but heroic effort of the struggle of the Maccabees. The Romans, as we all know, filled the minds of the young with the stimulating memories of ancestral triumphs; we have all, as schoolboys, read the story of the Roman matron encouraging her sons to their splendid—their almost hopeless—struggles for the liberties of the people, by recalling to them the achievement of the sires from whom they had sprung;

and few pictures of history are more touching, more instructive, than that of herself, when these very sons lay low,—triumphant though defeated,—living in her secluded home on the lofty promontory above the solemn sea, gazing on the mysteries of nature, interesting herself in the literary treasures of the geniuses of her time, but not so much mourning for the loss of her children, as sustaining her own waning spirit, and reviving the flagging energies of her declining days, by the recollection of their lofty character and their heroic deeds. Cornelia on the height of Misenum was strengthened *by an inspiring memory.*

And then, how much stronger is such a force upon a Christian! for indeed to the Christian pre-eminently "the memory of the just is blessed." Take, then, another instance from Christian history. You will recollect, no doubt, how St. Monica, in her last days, speaking to her son, whose conversion and whose greatness resulted from her own saintly life—her tears and prayers—said to him, "This only would I request, that you would *remember* me at the Lord's altar, wherever you be."[1] Doubtless she meant to ask the force of his prayers when the "sacrifice of our ransom" was offered, in pleading for her spiritual advance in the world of life beyond the grave; but her request would also bring to bear upon his own life in the future, the touching power of an undying memory, a memory

[1] Conf. B. ix. 27.

capable of stirring the affections and elevating the character; and in his case it did. We know from the confessions of that great father himself that in after times of struggles, toil, and teaching, the memory of the mother who through long years of sorrow had prayed for him with the supernatural force of a desperate desire, who had placed before his eyes an example of consistent saintliness—that *that* memory pierced his heart with purest sorrow, stirred his activities, and braced his flagging energies to the conflicts of life.

And so probably it has been, at least in some measure, with us all. I suppose there are few men of any real vigour of understanding, and certainly few of any depth of moral earnestness, who do not know what it is to have learned many lessons of self-restraint and courage from a memory. I imagine, my friends, that most of you—I might almost hope every one of you—when in the throes of temptation and doing battle with sin, have been able to fall back upon such a reserve of force as this suffices to supply. Life to some may have turned out to be a series of unfinished pictures, may have presented itself as a scrap-collection of works half done. You are pulled up in full career by sudden breaks, nay, before you yawn chasms, down which you gaze into a depth of such impenetrable darkness as dismays the startled soul. Some strain their tearful eyes over the silent surfaces of space, some yearn with aching hearts across the misty distances of years, and *there* they find the needed strength. Is it not so? When, at your ordinary work, you have been tempted to some sin, have you never known what it is to have had the great kind hand of God remove, it may be, the veil of sense, and bring back to you the vivid thought of one who is separated from you only by a few miles, but whom, present or separated, you love? or draw back, it may be, the curtain of the mystery of death, and flash upon you with appalling clearness the vision of some face, long loved, which you will never see on earth again?—some mother, brother, sister, friend, one with whose words the nerve of memory vibrates still, whose presence has left behind a sense of sweetness like the breath of flowers on a passing breeze in spring, whose sympathizing tenderness and consistent life had impressed upon you, almost with the force of palpable form, the solemn, the beautiful realities of another world? Has it been thus? If so, you have been supplied, in the hour of danger, with a sustaining force. Did you, coward, fail? Then sin committed has left its sting, envenomed with the added anguish of disloyalty to a friend. Did you succeed? Then these were your unspoken words, "I will *not* do the wrong, and I *will* do the right; and the reason stirring me to leave the one undone, and do the other, is nothing else than this, 'for thy dear sake.'" My friend, if you are ignorant of *that*, from my heart I pity you; you have failed to experience one of the purest and most powerful moral forces which has ever moved mankind;

I do not say the greatest or the highest, but certainly one, through which God works, and one of those forces with which, in her struggle for the education of society, Christianity can ill afford to dispense.

Well then, believe me, when a Christian succeeds, at any critical moment, in confessing the Lord, one great secret of the strength of the motive which moves him is that it has enlisted in its service the subduing power of *a most blessed memory*.

And what is the secret of such power? Ah me! there is one fact in all human history too common to arrest attention, too fearful to forget; one fact of tragic dignity and sorrow—the fact of the unrecurring Past. However bright the days of life, once gone they come no more. But what is *sad* of times and places, is *pathetic* when we speak of souls. That those we loved with passionate affection, and knew as intimately as we loved, should die, *should die*, should leave us, that *that* voice no more should thrill our souls with pleasure, *that* tread no more be heard upon the stairs, *that* laughter never again add joy to the life of the summer morning, *that* dear kind face not once more flash its rare sweet sunlight on our darkened day. Ah me! that "no more," "never more," with pitiless persistence comes as the heart-crushing cadence of a passing bell! When man realizes this, how can he bear it? He must satisfy his loving sorrow somehow, somewhere; those dear to him must not only live in another world, they must be immortal *here*, so what was dear in *them* lives, "for their sake," in *him*, in himself he strives to live as they would have done, as they would have had him do.

And more, he owed them much. Did he pay the debt while they were here? Alas! no. He has cried his tears of agony above the open grave, he has wailed his wail of repentance to the silent dead, but the grave made no rejoinder, there was no motion in the cold, the lifeless clay. What remains? Ah, God! little enough, but that little must be paid. He will *now* do as they *would have had* him once, he will make reparation for a neglected time. Longings for their immortality, longings for reparation for the past, these rise in one "pure image of regret," and become the leverage, the gigantic leverage, of a blessed memory, "I act for their sake." Is it not so? Have we not all known how sweet, how sad, how powerful is a memory? It is one of the sorrowful contradictions of our confused and tormented nature, that often, alas! the recollection of those who are gone acts more powerfully than the stimulus of their actual presence. How often a cold temper, a cruel antipathy, a hard unkindness, a selfish irritability, which would not yield to a dear living presence, are conquered by a pale face from the grave!

Well then, in the Christian too, there is something analogous,—the sense of the majesty, the beauty, the dearness of Christ, the sorrow of long neglect of all that tenderness, the hope to make that majestic life felt, because remade in his own soul, the secret springs of these affections—this hope and sorrow—are summed up in that phrase with which Jesus fires His servant's dying energies, "For My sake."

II. And again: the secret force of such a motive is not drawn merely from the past. A soul truly swayed by it is subdued by a *present influence*. I do not now pause to attempt any definition of so intangible an abstraction as influence, but I venture to remind you that there is no one of you who can possibly be quite without it; each of us exerts some influence over other lives; each, possessed of this in some measure, cannot possibly dispossess himself. Hence wide opportunities hence, too, grave responsibilities. But though such is the case, in some degree, in all, there are some men, as we know, who in every age have made their influence, in a pre-eminent degree, and with permanent effect, felt by mankind. Now, speaking for a moment of our Divine Master on the human side of His character, what were some of the secrets of that extraordinary influence exercised by Him in His earthly life?

The first was this—His exceptional power of human sympathy. Human sympathy, as we all know, enables us to feel not *for* but *with* men. Human sympathy may so place you upon the same platform, on the same level, side by side with your brethren, that you realize their sorrows, share their joys, and thrill with their emotions. And in proportion as it is so, you attract them to yourself by a wonderful, an indescribable attraction. Sympathy is one of those gifts—I may almost say one of those graces—which defies imitation. It cannot be counterfeited; it refuses to act as tool to expediency; it will not play the part of accomplice to a hypocrite. It may be cultivated, or the growth may be prematurely checked; like the poetic faculty, it cannot be made to order, it has its roots in the very fibres of our being. It is that majestic force by which the *human* in man readily and naturally prevails over the merely *accidental*, or *local*, or *transient*. Wherever it is, it is always beautiful, for, being inimitable, it is always true; and man, face to face with a moral beauty that he can feel, as well as comprehend, is as powerless to resist it as the needle to reject the magnet. Now this most beautiful of possessions was enshrined deeply, completely, in the nature of Him Who was the "First-born among many brethren."

But more than this is needed thoroughly to *move* men. For a sympathetic nature to benefit, in any high degree, those who feel its influence, it must be elevated by what, in ordinary men, we call the strength of sincere conviction. It is a truism to remark—none but dealers in paradox can deny—Christ, the human Christ, was transparently sincere. But it is none the less necessary to remember, He completed His influence on earth by His moral intensity. Those who have had clear and strong convictions, who have felt that the subject of those convictions was of vast, of lasting importance to mankind, in whom such feelings have been reinforced by the expansive power of sympathy—those are they who have *influenced* men, influenced them not in the region of outward circumstance merely, but in the immortal energies of their inner lives.

Now this illustrates the past and present work of our Divine Master. How is it, speaking humanly, that Christ exercised the influence which most assuredly He *did* exercise? It was by the force of just such a moral sublimity of character. And because as He was, so He is, because He has not only impressed upon the human family the image of His own unrivalled life, but lives and acts *now* by His Divine influence, as much as ever He did when visiting our earth, men are enabled in practical reality to shape and to restrain their actions "for His dear sake." To this influence each heart may open; and if so, how fruitful are the consequences! Yes, to this each heart *may* open. The Lord Jesus—you know it well—is no mere memory. He is a *present* Friend. From the history of His earthly work we *know* His human character; we *feel* its influence by His presence with us now. That character was too entirely beautiful to be *only* human, too universal to be restrained to one country or one time. Men felt it *ought* to be for ever, we know it *is*. Blessed Jesus! He is near us. The world drags us down, He lifts us to Himself. The mind disdains low motives under the influence of His presence. Can we content ourselves with selfish degradation when His appeal rings through us, "For My sake"?

The example of Jesus reproduced in the persons of His people is a force indeed. It has struck, it strikes the human family through every age and realm of Christendom,—by noble examples, and by saintly lives, —beneath lies one motive, the impulse of which they communicate to others—" For My sake."

Take courage then, for be well assured that the influence of one really Christian life—little as the world knows it, nor, till the judgment day, can know—is incalculably powerful. And here is its secret spring. In one sense it is born of the memory of a solemn Past, in another it springs from an active influence in the Present. The Christian cannot forget his Master's life of heroic fidelity to duty; he cannot ignore the invigorating influence of that dear, that mysterious presence; from both he draws inspiration for energy in action, and constancy in suffering,—" For His sake."

And so it is that the work of the Master is carried onward—He is felt, through souls He has chosen, in the world. Ah! my friends, the influence of Him Who " liveth and was dead" is felt, widely felt, in the ranks of humanity. It colours our politics, it tempers the heats of party passion, it projects rays of pure sunlight through the dense atmosphere of corrupt public opinion; it moulds in a measure the conventional usages of social life; it blunts the edge of envy; it quells the violence of rancour; it is like the fluctuating mystery of ocean waves which warm the icy wind and change it to a life-reviving breeze; it is like the glowing fire-shafts of the sun, which shape the densest clouds to splendid pictures; it is like the light of stars in an eastern sky, whose myriad rays combine in shedding a tender brightness through the chambers of the night. Half Christendom denies Christ, but Christ is *felt* in Christendom.

And here I must pause to face a not unusual objection. It is sometimes objected, that such a motive as this, in the England of the nineteenth century, is thinner than the shadow of a dream. We are told that it partakes too largely of sentiment; that it has too much to do with the *emotional nature*, really to impinge upon and force forward the character of man against the constant pressure of temptation. We are warned that men, because of their very manhood, cannot come out of the range and reach of the motives which play upon them more constantly, and with more concentrated strength, in daily life. This may be a protest against unreality, and if so indeed I respect it. The answer must be this; certainly, I grant that the motive of the text can only acquire its complete sovereignty by slow degrees. In its fulness, stimulating the feelings as well as bracing the will, it acts only upon the saints; but, my brothers, remember it does not act upon them because they are saints, but they become saints because it acts upon them. Remember that in early days of spiritual life, when a young man is converted to his God, when he wakens up to the meaning of the unending years, when he realizes the transient character of the Present, and the greatness and eternity of the Future that lies before him, when he is surprised into the acknowledgment of his dependence on another—on his God; at first, no doubt, he may *feel* a certain warmth of *feeling*, which dies down afterwards (who has not known it at such times of revival? who has not mourned its short-lived power?); at first he may not only feel an interest in the mystery and the majesty of Truth, but *feel* its exquisite beauty; and that feeling may become chilled again—for life is made, indeed, first of great impulses and then of falls; first perhaps of victories, and then of disappointments; first of a bright morning and then of a cloudy day;—but believe me that *this* too is, thank God! often the case: that though the morning has been bright, and then the day has been cloudy, the evening comes with a calm radiance which is better than that brightness, clearer from its contrast with the clouds, comes, in fact, to bring the promise of the eternal dawning.

Remember that first the soul begins after its conversion to love God with a warmth and enthusiasm which is chilled, alas! as it feels the fret, and the worry, and the weariness of life; then it may be it is arrested by the coldness of the world. Arrested did I say? No, not arrested. *Feeling*, after all, counts for little in religion —it is helpful, it is comforting, but *the* force is Will.

Feeling helped us to begin: it is gone in great measure, but it has left fact behind. Jesus *is* glorious, He *is* worth working for; we *know* it though we may not fully *feel*. Will is everything. *Act* on what once you *felt*. Love may be *effective* though not *affective*; to *do* as He would have you, though the *feeling* of enthusiasm may have abated in its warm young glow, is most truly to act " for His sake." But further, better days are before you; be true; keep face to face with the Eternal Truth, and you will not long resist its beauty; feeling deepened, purified, will at last return.

It is quite true, then, that such a motive will not act *in its fulness* at once—that it may be unreal to tell you to do everything from a conscious love (meaning a glowing *feeling* of affection) to Jesus Christ from the very first moment of your turning to Him in real surrender; that it may be impossible for you, in the senses, at every moment to recall that Divine vision, and to *feel* the warmth of that loving hand; but recollect that such truth only amounts to this, that you are living in an imperfect state, but a state advancing, and what just such a state requires, is to fall back upon a memory, to act on what it *knows*, not *feels*. Persevere, my brother, be faithful, be loyal, and you will advance (so the saints have shown us) until this spring of action becomes not only the force but the *joy* of the spirit's life. There is nothing unpractical in acting steadily upon what we *know* to be true, because at the moment we are not so sensitive to *the beauty* of the truth as once we were. But what in fact *is* meant is sometimes this, that men to be *men* must discard as visionary, the sublimer motives. This indeed is utterly, it is impudently false; it rests on a notion of manliness as untrue as it is injurious; it springs from the common fallacy that strength and unrestrainedness of passion are all one with strength of character. Worldliness, selfishness, baseness, or pettiness of motive are no proofs of practical manliness. Men flatter themselves by such convenient falsehoods, and I think that such flattery is bad. Young men of Manchester, mark my words: you are not strong, you are not vigorous, because you "see life," which means "see sin;" you are not practical or courageous, because you neglect your parents, sneer at sacraments, ignore your Bibles, or forsake your Church; you are not powerful and energetic and lords in God's creation, because you make a mock at religion or laugh at your Creator; you are not forcible in character, because you will not speak out for truth when others deride it. The worldling's taunt is neither clever nor uncommon; there is no manly vigour in threadbare and fifth-rate profanity. Such is not strength. If by "men" you mean those who most submit to the power of their passions; if by "men" you mean those who most submit to the strongest motives that prevail in the world around them, then forgive me for saying we use the phrase in different senses: these I call not "men," but "cowards." O my brothers, I am the last to be hard upon you, hard upon you when I love you (let me dare to use the apostle's language) "in the heart of Jesus Christ;" but I must boldly say to you, if such be your dream of human manliness, you are likely to become weak, or even effeminate. It is weakness that is unable to grasp a sublime motive; it is effeminacy that succumbs before the strength of passion or the mere voice of a passing world. The objection has no force to me, because therein I recognise a deep and terrible fallacy; and the fallacy is this—a confusion between a force attacking and a force defending a citadel. Every soul must conquer its passions or be conquered by them. A strong soul is the one that by grace subdues them, and it is confusing together different things, it is false and misleading, to imagine that force of ungoverned passion means force of character. Quite the reverse.

This is evident in a moment. It is easy to sin; it is hard to resist; hard to be brave for the truth; hard to be honest in conviction; hard to be sincere in thought; hard to scorn a lie; hard to trample on reputation; hard to stand up amongst your fellows and witness to God: hard, my brother; ay, but when you "endure hardness" and do your duty, *that* is force of character, a different thing altogether from force of passion. And real and lasting force of character is sustained, depend upon it, by a pure, a lofty motive.

Of course it is true enough that such a motive can have no power over the lives of men, if they deliberately shut their lives against it. How may we come within its range? How but by guarding or recovering purity of heart. Christ teaches us that the "pure in heart . . . see God." A pure life keeps a character strong, because it withdraws it from the paralyzing play of the passions, and it keeps the heart tender, because it empties it of *self.* It is *then* indeed that the nature is open to lofty influences.

Guard purity of heart and life "for His dear sake," and then you will be increasingly open to this ennobling motive, because you will be increasingly capable of a real love. For indeed though our senses are the channels of emotion, love is not of the senses but of the soul; it is the strong man who is capable of it, for it is he who is tender because it is he who is pure. Indeed it is true that such an appeal has no power to reach the heart of a sentimental dreamer. It is a motive for those who are earnestly struggling in the fierce battle of life.

There are in Holy Scripture three instances which make clear the need and value of a lofty motive in the ordinary duties and temptations of life. You remember Joseph when he was exalted to the first place in the financial direction of Egypt—at that time the greatest monarchy of the world—you remember how, amidst the magic splendours of that wonderful nation, after a rise unparalleled in its extraordinary degree and rapidity, and a position giddy in its vast height—you remember how, after all, his love showed itself so strong and powerful and tender to the old father who came down to him to die. But what had been the history of that loving heart? It had been kept fresh by purity. There had been fierce temptation, and at the turning-point—when his whole future character was trembling in the balance, when to yield was so easy, to conquer so hard—he turned upon the tempter with the power of a mighty motive. Was *that* motive such as the world would think "*practical*"? But practical and effective it was in the soul of that young man. " How can I," he said, " do this great wickedness, and *sin against God?* "

Follow on along this line of Hebrew history till you come to David. Here at any rate you have a man of a force of passion so frightful that at times he was altogether conquered by the strength of his desires; but if, alas! he did not resist temptation, at least he returned to penitence. Sweetest of characters, even in the hours of his sinning, his *heart* was always right. And what was it, what was the motive, powerful enough to revive the desire of better things in that poor fallen man?

It was no practical motive of self-interested regret. It was one supposed too high for ordinary life; it was a loving thought of God—"against *Thee*, *Thee* only have I sinned, and done this evil in *Thy* sight."

I mention one more. In the period of transition from the old Jewish faith to Catholic Christianity, there is no more remarkable figure than that of the young man Stephen. You remember how he was taken out from amongst others to do a common work, a work requiring practical capacity, but also—for it was the management of the widows' fund in the difficulties of the early Church—requiring a degree of real tenderness and thought; and how that character developed. Look at the critical moment when he came to die; at least you see the strength of a hero, and the tenderness of a saint. He was young, like any of you, but he faced his enemies, refused all suggestions of surrendering the truth which had been given him to hold; but prayed with a yearning heart for those who murdered him, and "fell asleep," crushed indeed with the cruel stones, but with his face "like an angel."

What moved him? His life was commonplace enough; and with something like brutal fury he was hustled to his death. What moved him? How did he resist? How stand? Some useful worldly motive? I trow not. It was love of Jesus, it was "for His dear sake."

And after all these were but men. And the spiritual forces under which they acted, may be felt and used by ourselves.

Indeed it is a libel on humanity, to speak as though men in ordinary life must be impervious to the action of noble and supernatural motives. Man is both a moral and a spiritual being. Every man you meet *has* a conscience, and *is* a living soul. He may be crusted over so thick with conventional varnish, he may be so completely enslaved by the Commonplace, that it is hard to reach the man *himself*. He may be almost buried alive under the weight of his wealth, or the splendour of his titles, or the accumulated rubbish of his habitual sins, but don't be scared by all these appearances; he is *himself* somewhere underneath it all. Forget the accidental, remember the essential. He is *a soul*, he must live; what is more, at last he must die. He is a spirit, and his heart admits by the necessary condition of this very nature, of being laid open to the penetrating forces of a spiritual power. If his whole being is ever really to be moved, it must be by some motive capable of piercing him to the very core of his soul. Is there such? It may seem impossible, but grace is mighty, and the most ordinary man is an immortal, and the love of Jesus is a force indeed. If once, oh, if once wakened to the facts of his hope and his history, he may yet yield to that most piercing motive, "for My sake."

III. But more than all our Lord's appeal is to *personal affection*. To do anything "for sake of another" evidences love. And if in any measure we *do* love Jesus Christ, it is because He "first loved us." To love is at all events a high affection, a purifying power: it means self-renunciation, it means a life outside ourselves more precious to us than our own. To love Jesus Christ is a high thing indeed. It is possible only by Divine assistance; only also for one whose eyes are open to the Unseen; only to a mind grasping truth and touched by its beauty, in a world of falseness and shadow. Truly, to see Him is a great grace, but, having seen, it is impossible not to love.

But love for an unseen Master has many degrees: it sweeps through many meridians of spiritual attainment, from the burning ecstasy of seraphs to the frail but real longings of some yearning soul. It is a work of the Spirit; but it begins in the mind with some sense, some realization of our own need and His goodness. We cannot withhold some gratitude. What do we not owe Him? Morally, He has made for us a new world. To live a member of His Church, instead of in the ancient civilization, is like escaping from the biting frosts of the frozen ocean to the sunlight and blue seas and skies of Italy. He has shown us the *real* meaning and horror of sin, and not only the awfulness but the beauty of holiness. What do we not owe Him? We have in us the witness of a sense of the majesty of right, and a witness of our weakness and rebellion. He has come, He has shown and fulfilled that deep mystery, the need of which is *felt* in all awakened souls, the influence of which is not limited to the life of the creature, but extends to the destinies of eternity—the mystery of Atonement, the virtue of perfect obedience, the power of the Precious Blood.

And this for *us*. It is when aroused to that truth, so mysterious, yet so suited to our needs, nay, so evidently *the* necessary power and consolation for which we long, that the soul is enabled to correspond to such immensity of blessing, and to act, or abstain from acting, by the strong power of a sincere affection, "for His sake."

The power of such a motive on our own souls must, I need hardly say, depend upon the place we assign, and the value we attach to the life and work of Jesus Christ.

Upon the place and work of any man, and the acceptance of that place and work in the minds of others, depends his influence. If a feeling so warm and so urgent as that which is implied in the appeal of Jesus Christ is to move the human heart, such a feeling must itself have a substantial foundation. I do not insult you by inviting you to act upon a mere shadowy sentiment. No, this rests upon a sturdy truth. Such a motive to have power must rest upon a solid conviction. And one reason why Christian motive is often painfully ineffective in these days, is because the minds of Christian men are so darkened and overshadowed by the cloudy atmosphere of unbelieving thought. It seems almost impossible for men in these days—speaking humanly—to grasp strongly, hold firmly, act upon practically, and literally believe, *any* supernatural truth; for our literature, and therefore our thoughts, are haunted with the enfeebling spectres of sceptical dreams. Oh may He rise—the true Sun of the morning—and shed

His light on the clouded hearts, and restore the vigour of a sincere conviction. Christianity means conviction; and where conviction is, there is a basis on which motive may rest.

(1.) The motive of the text has power over hearts in which three important truths are grasped with sincere conviction. That motive is a *demand* and an *appeal*. It is a demand that can only be made by right of one title, it is such as any other fails altogether to justify. To ask any human being to alter his life, to tone his conduct, to regulate his thoughts, to restrain his words, " for sake of " another, must imply a well-founded claim of that other, upon his affections and thought, or else such a demand could only be treated with the disregard it deserves. But to expect attention to such a prayer from men separated by long expanses of space, and widening tracts of intervening years, could only be the mental attitude of a madman, unless it were the exercise of the right of God. You must either treat it as an amusing impertinence, or meet it with a tribute of adoring love. Christ is God, "Light of Light," "God of God," "Very God of Very God," from all eternity to all eternity consubstantial with the Father, one and everlasting in that Divine nature, and by that right and that alone, He is the Being to summon me across the ages and say, "Do it for My sake." That sublime, that beautiful motive has its full power upon those alone who have surrendered —surrendered wholly—to the claims of that conviction.

(2.) The recollection of His true humanity is equally important, because it is from a *human* voice on Calvary that there comes, not a demand, but an appeal—" My child, because I am what I am, the Man of men, the Head of your humanity; because as man you must love men, love Me, the highest and greatest, and do all for My sake."

(3.) There is a third truth, to be thoroughly impressed with which is to allow such a motive to have its full play. It is that truth which Paul so grasped that it transformed his life—not that there is sin outside in the world, but that there is sin within your own heart; not that Jesus came to save from some indefinite danger beyond yourself, but that sin being *in* the human will, He came to save you from *your own* sin; not that He came to die for a world which you can imagine as a great fact lying beyond you, but the more affecting truth, that because He died for the world, therefore for *every* sinner in it—the truth represented by the cry of the apostle, " He loved *me*, and gave Himself for *me*." Because He loved *you*, therefore you can answer as the Apostle John teaches us—" We love Him because He first loved us." Grasp that result of the Incarnation in your toil, in your temptation. Look up and remember the fact that He loved and loves *you*, and you may yet say humbly, but with real truth, " Then, my Lord, I will fight against the sin within me, and around me, for the love of Jesus, for Thy sake."

Now one word of the effect. Effects, of course, are produced by forces, whether in nature or in grace. It is a law—resulting from one of the last great "generalizations" of science, as it is called, the "conservation of force"—it is a law, that the effects are produced not only from the amount but from the suitable distribution of force. And it seems to me that in the supernatural life there is a parallel law. Effects will be very different according to the degree in which the action of such a motive as this is permitted, and according to the antecedent condition of the character upon which it is brought to bear. But these are general effects, which indeed may be expected wherever it is at work. If, remembering Jesus as He was, and knowing that He is so now; if, grasping the truth of His Godhead and Manhood, and realizing the personal relation of your own soul to Him, you allow your action to be governed by the great thought and great memory of Him, then I am convinced that one effect will be certain to follow—*you will view things increasingly and more distinctly from His point of view.*

The world will tell you that practically there has been no real corruption of humanity. Christ tells you that He came to repair man's shattered fortunes. The world will tell you that practically this life is intended for us to seek and find our personal satisfaction. Christ will tell you that *self-sacrifice* is the source at once of power and happiness. The world will tell you that the legitimate range of human action can only be measured by the force of human passion. Christ will tell you that no human passion is worthy of a creature who comes from the hand of the Divine Artist, till it has been purified and elevated by restraint and correction. And if you allow this loving motive to act upon you, your outlook will be from Christ's point of view, and you will act accordingly. It is here that the value of such a motive is felt in a state—like our modern life—of complex and confusing civilization. It is *the* corrective to a merely easy-going Christianity. "The world"—the unsupernatural twist and temper of minds set upon the present—always hates, always will hate, Jesus Christ. Woe to those who think it otherwise, and enter upon the Christian course with a reverse expectation! Excitement, interest in what is new, the taste, the incipient taste, of joy which is sure to be felt from *any* connection with Him, carries them on a certain distance. But opposition comes. Their "views" (for in such cases there are only "views," not beliefs) soon fade and grow sad and dim. They are filled with fear, renounce good practices, and at last publicly deny their Master. Pitiful backsliders! They have lost a spiritual power, and the completeness and crown of a heavenly character. Persecution has fallen upon them, and "by-and-by" they have been "offended." What is the secret? The real motive—with all their warm feelings and enthusiastic devotion—their real motive is *self*, not *Christ*. They are without that permanent form of grace—*the* Christian motive, "for My sake."

A further effect is this. A soul under the sway of this motive has gained *the secret power by which to soften down the harder lines of life.* Some lives only thrive in the sunlight, can only grow in the midst of happiness and blessing, and when they have to go out into a world of toil and struggle, the weariness and the worry check their growth. How are the hard lines to be softened? where is the power to bring back the old strength again? It comes with the rising of the Morning Star. It wakes with the dawning of the Sun of Righteousness. It is Christ revealed within you—the Hope of Glory. He opens a new, a beautiful world within you by joy at the thought of His tender devotion—"My child, I loved you—is not that enough to make life blessed?" and you can look up in your sorrow and say, "Yea, dear Lord, for Thy sake."

These are true effects, effects which have been produced in men; they have; and they have transformed life. In the old mediæval story of the brother and sister who met on the Apennines in the rugged pass, who, in presence of the watching mountains and before the witness of the silent sea, determined to part for ever because each had a work for God; in the agony of tears and embraces, in the strong crying and sadness of that supreme moment, when souls that have loved, and loved deeply and tenderly, are rent asunder for a lifelong separation, in that story, symbolical of so many sorrows travelled through, never forgotten by human souls, sorrows such as we may have to go through before our mortal pilgrimage is done, the subduing force of an uncomplaining resignation may still be, "for the love of Jesus," "for His sake."

The motive has made men strong, and therefore it may make you. It may help you in your life, in your struggle, in your toil, in your quiet moments, in your secluded hours, as in the busy and noisy streets of this great commercial capital; it may help you when others are around you, when their worldliness or wickedness is beating your spirit down; it will help you when the scene is dark and weary; it will help you when you are inclined to be lazy and cannot rise in the morning and say your prayers; it will help you when you are slothful and evade the duty of going to church; it may help you when you are cold and disinclined to prepare for the Sacrament; it may help you when sensual thoughts come over you, and your higher, better self is dragged down, and the tempter says to you that *that* evil thing is not unworthy of a man; it will help you if you will turn to Him and cry to Him, "O my Lord, my Jesus, I will, or I will not, for Thy sake."

And one most telling outcome of such a motive has been the extent and depth of self-sacrificing effort visible in corporal works of mercy since Christ came. For how moving, how stimulating is the thought that those who feed the hungry, console the sorrowing, sustain the fainting, visit the sick, "inasmuch as they have done it unto one of the least of these" His "brethren, have done it unto" Him! Unselfish, pitying, loving effort is ever fruitful "for His sake."

"*For His sake!*" In a word, it is the spring of energetic life, whenever, in works however commonplace and unattractive, we so carry the thought of Him enshrined within our souls, that all we do or leave undone is consciously (or half unconsciously, because habitually) referred to Him, as our Standard, our Comfort, our Judge.

"*For His sake!*" It is the central motive. Look at any man moved by it. Look at any, young or old. What do you see? My friends, the saintly painter Angelico flung out his thoughts upon the cells of San Marco, and those who visit Florence are arrested and subdued by the purity of his dreams. My friends, that other powerful artist who adorned the ceiling of the Sistine, has traced out figures copied more directly from the study of the human form, but warmed into life by the fire of divine genius; and of such men we cannot but say that they penetrated the hidden chambers of another world, before they could leave before the eyes of five astonished centuries, such visions, more lovely or more appalling than the mysteries and marvels of our dreams. But I tell you that in the streets of London, in the streets of Manchester, it is possible for us in our ordinary life to see pictures more pure than the dreams of Augelico, more powerful than the masterpieces of Angelo. Here we are face to face with living men, some in youth, in the early days of passion and struggle, some in age, when the fire is failing and the eye growing dim, who, in the midst of a world that forgets God, or defies Him, are enabled to do mighty things though hidden, to sustain an inner life of loyalty to supernatural principle, amidst the fretting care of daily toil.

What is the secret force of their character? what the purifying power in their life of struggle? They have realized the greatness and seriousness of humanity from the life and Passion of Jesus Christ. Human misery and human glory are more clearly traced in their thoughts than the structure of the human form on the canvas of Angelo; *and* they have seen into eternity, and there, face to face with the mysteries of human sorrow, is a diviner vision than the dream of Angelico—the face of Jesus Christ. Life is changed. What is the purpose of this passing dream? What are the virtues of these fleeting hours? One virtue, one purpose—to impress that image on a sorrowing world, to carry out the objects of that life, to fill all work with supernatural power—for a supernatural motive, "for His sake."

Dwell then, dwell recurringly, habitually, on the thought of Jesus Christ. Low aims, distorted views, self-pleasing desires, selfish struggles yield before that vision of self-sacrificing love; the mere recollection of our Master has a kind of sacramental power. Read and re-read His life in the Gospels, dwell on His constant nearness and unabated claim; think of it, and pray till it illumines and restrains your daily conduct, with the bright sense of His blessed presence, and the severe exactions of His holy law.

So will life grow in fruitfulness and power, *each* act of daily duty acquire an eternal significance, till He Who advanced the claim, recognise your loyalty of submission, and by His merits ye "have right to the tree of life, and enter within the gates to the city."

SERMON IX.[1]

For the Glory of God.

"Whether therefore ye eat, or drink, or whatsoever ye do, do all to the glory of God."—1 CORINTHIANS x. 31.

WE reach to-day the third and most solemn aspect of Christian motive. And I have preferred throughout to speak of *aspects* of one great motive, rather than of three distinct springs of action, because it seems to me that in doing so I am respecting facts. To learn the love of man because, by the law of Christ, it is revealed to us that man is a fitting subject for a Christian's sympathy, and at least *may* be truly lovable, drives us back, of course, into the examination of the claims of Jesus—the Lord, the Lawgiver, the Representative of the race—upon our own personal affection; and that, further, must carry the mind into deeper depths of eternity, where it may track to its origin the cause of that claim put forth in the active life of Christ, by endeavouring to interpret His essential nature; or, in other words, to learn to love man truly, we require the stimulus of the love of the best and greatest—the love

[1] Preached also in substance in St. Thomas', Regent Street, London, in December 1877.

of Jesus; and to love our Redeemer is to conform the springs of our action to the forces that stimulated His, that is, to find our ultimate basis of motive in "the glory of God." The governing Christian *motive*, expressed in terms of its ultimate spring and essential character, is, then, "the glory of God."

Well now, first of all, I would ask you to notice how the practical importance of such a motive is indicated by the *manner* in which it is presented in the text. There is always a danger of a revulsion of the human mind against even the mere statement of so high a motive, and that danger is intensified amongst ourselves from our own national character. You will remember the *on dit* that went abroad some years ago, that the sovereign of a great nation, with which England was then at war, had flattered himself with hopes of success in the struggle by sneering at Englishmen as a mere "nation of shopkeepers." Whether or not it be true that the then Czar of Russia actually uttered the words, the mere report of such a saying contained a lesson and a warning. It represented, on the one hand, the fact, of which we need not be the least ashamed, that Englishmen, for the most part, are sensitive in their fear of anything not evidently useful, are somewhat morbidly suspicious of what may appear exaggerated or overstrained; that they instinctively shrink from what is purely and merely transcendental; that they try to value things rather at what they deem their practical value. But that there should be a colour of truth in such a sneer reminds us also of a national as well as human danger; the danger that we all as human creatures—and above all as Englishmen—may acquire a vicious habit of appraising things simply by their market value, of always asking first, "How will they work?" It represents to us the fact, therefore, that, though certainly it is true that we ought to be on our guard against mere transcendentalism, ought to be suspicious of that which belongs apparently only to the world of ideas, and does not touch the world of facts, yet that, at the same time, that kind of rough and ready manner in matters Divine may become, in truth, the deepest affectation; that men who are always professing to look at the greatest mysteries, and at the darkest solemnities of Divine faith—at the loftiest facts transcending thought yet touching human destiny—in what they are pleased to call a "practical" fashion, are very often led astray through shallowness of thought, or suffer from a painful deficiency of moral earnestness. We must be on our guard against shrinking back from all high motive, as if it were mere idealism. Englishmen, it may be truly said, are energetic and practical; but Englishmen have to watch against their great temptation to forsake the world of ideas altogether, have to remember that to state an idea truly is only to give an accurate account of the basis of material fact.

Now, the way in which St. Paul puts the truth of the

text brings before us the eminently practical nature of this apparently most ideal motive. Not indeed that *that* is directly and at first sight the point to be observed. The question we ought to ask ourselves in all such cases is, not one as to the practical success or "working" of the thing, not "Is it practical?" but "Is it true?" and if it be true, then further, we have to go on, not to endeavour to conform it to our shallow practice, but to conform our ordinary habits to that high and true canon presented as the ideal and standard of life.

However, St. Paul presents the great Christian motive, in a way sufficiently evidencing at once its working value and its truth. The Corinthians, you will remember, were in a practical difficulty. Social life had been upheaved by the action of Christianity. Like the shuddering of the sunny, peaceful plains of Campania from the fierce shock of the insurgent fires of Vesuvius, the whole social fabric, wherever Christ's hand had touched it, was in a state of convulsive trembling; and the convulsion was felt in the agonies of its rebound alike in the deepest and most trivial things of life. The ordinary gentleman of the day, in Corinth, was no longer able to associate himself with his everyday acquaintances in the pleasures or the business of social life, without the rebuking face of the new religion gazing at him in serious warning, amid the revelries of the crowd. He could not, as we should say, "dine out" with his friend without being at once confronted by a practical difficulty. The old idol-worship had interpenetrated the social life of Corinth, and when Christians came to accept the invitation of their friends to an ordinary social entertainment, they were placed in a serious dilemma, as they could not but appear to sanction by their presence a service of idols and an insult to God, or else would be forced to cut themselves off from the commonest demands of the society of the time. Now, certainly St. Paul in his usual manner touches specific dangers with specific remedies; but at the same time he never, I venture to say, limits himself to such a method, but invariably (whatever be the difficulty he has to deal with) he goes beyond the exact line of the particular question and its corresponding remedy, and sketches out a serviceable and yet comprehensive canon of conduct. Thus, feeling that what is a desirable principle for *all* converts, when they have seceded from heathenism to the Christian Church, is some guidance for those at Corinth how to comport themselves properly in their social entertainments, instead of going into all the wearisome intricacies of the difficulty—although he *does* touch them also when necessary—he lays down the comprehensive rule of the text. Possibly at first sight you may call it unpractical, but when his meaning is clearly seen, it is, I think, eminently to the point. "Therefore, whether ye eat, or drink, or whatsoever ye do," —the rule for you is this,—" do all to the glory of God."

My friends, I submit that in laying down such a rule,

St. Paul is supplying to Christian conduct a motive at once practical and true. Well, the first question before us is, "What did St. Paul *mean?*" Remember how important it is firmly to demand an answer to that question. The risk we often run in interpreting Holy Scripture is, that with our traditional reverence for the Bible, and our long-formed habits of listening to its sacred words, and rightly, as of exceptional value, and our deeply-rooted prejudices as to its necessary and accepted sense, we may become essentially superstitious and unreasonable in our Bibliolatry, fail to fathom the real meaning of any passage, but take some isolated verse without serious reference to its context, and so miss completely its *meaning*. It is in that way the doctrine of the Church on Holy Baptism has been denied by the misinterpretation of one text in St. John. It is in that way that the harmony of the truth has been disturbed, and therefore the growth of spiritual life impoverished, by the narrow and meaningless interpretation put upon the apostle's exhortation to the startled and anxious jailer at Philippi. This is often treated as an encouragement to some mysterious feat of spiritual athletics, whereby he was once and for ever rescued from ruin, instead of a simple statement of the fact that Christianity, not Heathenism, is the path of safety, and a belief in the Lord Jesus as the Saviour of the sinner the one reasonable and blessed consequence of the awakening of a soul to truth. Alas! the failure of an earnest spirit of inquiry has often induced serious and honest men to turn wearily aside from all examination of the higher motives of Christian conduct, as if they had nothing to do with practical life. What did St. Paul *mean?*

Well, at any rate his words are an expression of a fundamental truth of religion, the truth, namely, that while the living God is the source and efficient cause of all things, so also He is their final end; the truth, therefore, that God (though He gives lavishly to man gifts of help, and comfort, and blessing) is Himself, and not anything He gives, man's final and only satisfaction; and therefore, that the end He had in view in His creation, and has in view in His government, of the world, is not at all that He Himself may receive from any external being or thing a support which is never needed by that majestic self-sufficing life, but that He may have about Him numberless sons, like unto Himself in goodness and beauty, and finally fitted to be partakers of His own beatitude and glory; and if this truth, as to the final object of life, and therefore the final cause of God's action in Christ Jesus, and government of the world, underlay the apostle's thought,—as I think it did,—what must be the result? Surely nothing else but the statement of the text. For if there be such a fundamental fact of religion, what is, what *must* be the object of man's highest efforts but to conform in all things to that necessary truth? Our moral nature teaches us the need that each is in, to be true to himself; and that is—as every religious man knows—to be true to the intention of God.

But mark, when I say "to be true to himself," I touch upon a majestic and an awful attribute of our nature, which, indeed, is one of the deepest of mysteries, but one of the most incontrovertible of facts, which also we never can put out of court when we take stock of the riches of our immortal life, in relation to God—our own, our individual liberty. My friends, we are apt to call man "the puppet of circumstances;" we are apt to look upon him as though he were tossed about as a fragment of wreckage on a capricious sea, as if he were dragged like a captive at the wheels of a Roman conqueror, as the unwilling and helpless slave of passion; we are apt to look at man as if outward influences had him completely at their command, to drive hither and thither in helpless impotence. There is a certain amount of truth in such a philosophy of despondency, but for the most part statements of this kind are metaphorical, or at least incomplete. Man is never altogether the puppet of circumstances. Man is never completely the slave of passion. Man is never a merely helpless victim of flowing and receding currents; he is never necessarily the merely submissive slave of what is passing and external. Man always has within him, in the ultimate seat of his being, within his own *essential* life, a majestic, self-determining force, and there must be some coalescing of that force with the external influence, before such influence can possibly turn him to good or evil. Whether that external influence be the grace of God, attracting and assisting him to glory, or whether it be the temptations of sense, seducing him to the degradations of sin, man is free, majestically free. Liberty is the attribute of our magnificent, our awful nature. It is not pretended of course for a moment that the whole subject is free from difficulties; certainly it is not. *How* such amplitude of freedom is consistent with the almighty sway of an all-surveying Mind is, in our present state of probation, an insoluble mystery. But there are certain first truths of our being which can only be gainsaid at peril of mental or moral suicide. We are conscious that we are free. And because it is so—it is a fair question to ask—how *ought* man to act in order to be true to his nature? It is a fair general answer to say, he ought freely to will in conformity to that truth. But alas! his will, though free, is weak; Christian Revelation, however, brings the promise, and the Christian Church possesses the machinery for supplying needed help. And therefore the Christian, if acting in conformity to his higher nature, and by the power of the grace that is given, is sure to act as the text describes; it is the practical outcome of his actual circumstances and of his relation to the living God. "Whatsoever ye do, do all to the glory of God."

"What, then, is glory?" The answer may be given

in two forms, for glory may be objective or subjective; in plain English, may be viewed in the Being Himself, or in its effect upon the relation of others to Him. The "glory" of any living being, then, is the internal or the external excellency of it, by which it is worthy of acquaintanceship, and love, and praise. Or again, glory is the reputation and love and praise accorded to, felt for, that object or being, because of its excellency. Now you know, "to *do all* to the glory of God," must be the free act of man in relationship to God's inner excellence, or essential glory, which is worthy of exciting in the creature a desire of closer acquaintance, and a limitless offering of love and praise.

Is it possible to know anything of God's essential excellence so that we may "*do* all for His glory"? Is it, in fact, possible to be "acquainted with God"? To say nothing of the unvarying witness of the moral sense, suggesting to us an ideal and standard of absolute goodness; to say nothing of the clear indication of the necessary excellence of Divine character, given to man in the revelation of the decalogue; to say nothing of the pointed exhortation of the prophet, "Acquaint thyself with God, and be at peace,"—we can learn of His glory, and "*do* all" according to that knowledge, from the testimony of two witnesses accessible to every child of man.

I. The first is Creation; you have looked at it—have you not?—for many years, day by day. Alas! it is one thing to *look at* an object, another to *observe* its teaching.

You have plenty of opportunities of seeing the exact conformity of nature to the uniform requirements of law. The majestic march of the planets—sure, stately, yet of bewildering swiftness—measuring immensity; the beauty of the simplest visions of daily experience —the breaking of the dawn, the dreamy brightness of the noon, the falling shadows of evening, the glory of the solemn hoary winter day, the glow of summer, the bursting of the flowers, the sparkling of the early dew, the graceful curvature of the valleys, and sharp clear outline of the rising hills—those exquisite touches of nature's pencil that every eye can see in the fresh portfolios of the coming seasons, in gloom or in brightness, storm or sunny calm,—these are but many voices, many pictures of unalterable and fruitful fact. "The heavens declare the glory of God; and the firmament showeth His handiwork. Day unto day uttereth speech, and night unto night showeth knowledge. There is no speech nor language, where *their* voice is not heard." Creation witnesses to Divine excellence, for though the death-veil is "cast over all people, and spread over" the face "of all nations," and though "the whole creation groaneth and travaileth in pain together," yet it is evident that these spectres of darkness and sorrow are something alien to the purpose of this beautiful world; and itself, in the beauty which is its natural and congenial accompaniment, is witness of the excellence behind, in Him Who made it all.

II. My brethren, there is one other book in which you can read the excellency of God. Creation is wonderful; Incarnation is more so. The earthly life of our Divine Master reveals to us a world of moral and spiritual loveliness, more exquisite in beauty, more penetrating in power, than anything that appears in physical creation. I have ventured to call the motive—"love of Jesus"—the central in the trilogy, and indeed it leads us to the lower, "love for man," as well as to the higher, "the glory of God." The soul is attracted by the tender sympathy and moral grandeur of the human Christ, and learns more earnestly to love a race of which He is "the Firstborn," and individual souls, with whom He has deigned to identify Himself; but it is when the soul realizes the further truth that Jesus is God, that it wakens in wonder and love to the truth, that it is in that *human* character of such unearthly nobleness it has to learn the inner life of its Maker, in its beauty, its gentleness, its sweetness, its tenderness, its strength. For this reason it is that the Incarnation as an unveiling of God, as a teaching of truth, as a stimulus to spiritual life, is so vastly valuable, besides its supreme importance in the great work of redemption, through the mystery of the Passion. You can be "acquainted with God," you can read in creation, you can read in the incarnate Christ, His character and His power; and thus it is, that the illuminated soul of the creature has some faint but true glimpse of "the glory of God."

But further, to be "in Christ" is to be "a new creature." Old things pass away, all things become new. The new creation! Fresh and purified affections, a strong, an invigorated will, newly-discovered regions for the exercise of thought, a landscape of unutterable, unearthly loveliness, unfolded before the spiritual vision —what is this but a deepening union of the soul with the Uncreated? What is this but Christ revealed *in* the regenerated creature? What is this but that "life eternal" which consists in the knowledge of God?

What follows? Supposing that a man does "acquaint" himself " with God," then—who can deny it?—that soul *must* love Him. Oh! to think that there are men in this world who in no sense love God, is to waken up to the truth, that there are men in this world who are walking with purblind eyes in the midst of a temple of majesty and glory; it is to waken up to the fact, that they have no eyes for the real sense of creation; nay more, for the unapproachable moral and spiritual beauty of the life of Jesus; for to *see* what is beautiful is, by the necessity, by the privilege of that great nature within us, to *love* it, and thus, to be "acquainted with God," is to proceed to love God, and what is this but more and more to enter into the mystery of His glory?

Anything more? I answer—one thing at least. What is the outcome of the love of the creature? My friends, the outcome of anything substantial, of anything that has within it an energy of life, is sure to appear in some vivid fashion, plain to the eye, or at least intelligible to the mind. The thunder-clouds, when they roll through the heaven to battle, strike forth before the eye the vividness and the beauty of the lightning; the rolling masses of the sea at night,—driven by the wind, and lying beneath the brightness of the summer moon,—as they dash up here and there against the ship's side, show a fringe of phosphorescent fire; and what that phosphorescence is to the mass of waters, and what the lightning is to the blocks of clouds, such is the praise of the creature in the energy and activity of his joy and thankfulness, and bursting forth from the fire and the fulness of His love. To be acquainted with God is to love Him; to love Him is to set the heart a-singing one voiceful or voiceless pæan of rejoicing, giving "glory, laud, and honour" to the living God. To be acquainted with, to love, to praise the Eternal,—in whatever details of life these inner actions are called into activity, whether in great things or in little,—that is "to do all to the glory of God."

Love is energetic and expansive; it desires that its object should be understood and loved. Its expression, in praise, will be such, and so directed, as to attain this end. In proportion to its depth and truth, it will exhibit before other minds, and other lives, the beauty of its object by every means. Therefore the creature, loving God, will be proclaiming in his own soul, and before angels and men, the character and beauty of the

Creator. Of this the external, partial expression will be *Praise*; hence the unflagging worship of the Church in every age: the consistent constant testimony will be in the *life*; hence the miracles of self-forgetting in the annals of the saints. To do all things in view of God's goodness, impelled by an enthusiastic homage of His greatness and beauty, with the inward settled sense,—sometimes consciously felt, but always, consciously or unconsciously, *there*,—is "to do all for the glory of God." Never forget this, man is a social being; he is not simply self-sufficing, without some power of responsible choice; he must have one of two objects predominantly before him—self or God; according to *which* is prevailing, he acts for his own glory or for God's.

And further, in conformity to the prevailing attraction he is sure to act in the serious crises of life, which test his bent and force of character, and therefore it is *in* these crises that the strength of motive may be measured.

Take two instances. When you stand, my brethren, on the top of the Capitol, and gaze over the ruins of the former Forum of Rome, you see before you the outward sign of the inward truth—a civilization in collapse; and when before your fancy rise once more the crowds of moving, teeming presences, which people the interspaces of the Roman Past, there are few, perhaps, that more conspicuously present themselves, than the shadowy form of the great orator who used to move those masses of men in the Forum by his finished and fiery eloquence.

Some of you will remember the great crisis of that man's life; he was driven into exile; and, unnerved and broken, he solaced himself, if so I may say, by cries of anguish and distress. When the daughter whom he loved so dearly was taken from him, he beat himself about angrily against the bars of life, like a scared and impotent bird in a confining cage, and could find no consolation, no interior peace. And, finally, when there came the collapse of the commonwealth, when he had to face in full view the tragic fate of that which he had dearly loved, and for which he had in his manner toiled,—searching for something on which to rest, all seemed chaos and despair.

Stand again for a moment outside the walls of Rome, and contemplate another picture. Before you stretches the Ostian Way; you can see it crossing the many-coloured, undulating distances of the dim Campagna, away over wild reaches and desolate tracts, under flitting cloud, or burning sunlight, past sleeping convent, or dead and mouldering ruin, always, like a weary traveller, wandering dreamily onwards towards Ostia and the sea. On that road, some eighteen centuries past, another great man, also (at least by right accorded to him) a Roman, had met the final crisis of his destiny. He too was no mean orator, he too had a powerful mind, a vivid imagination, an energetic, affectionate, yearning heart—another crisis he had passed through in his life, when all the world holds dear was lost, the crisis of his conversion. What was it that upheld him then? He had counted all as nothing for "the glory of God," that he might "win Christ." A further crisis came, the crisis of the sorrows of churches that he had been building up and teaching. Where did he look? Upwards and with constancy, only praying that they might be strengthened by "the riches of the glory of God." Then came this final crisis, when he stood almost alone; when the old man, having fought his fight and done his work, at last had to face the dreadfulness of desertion in death; and yet, when "Paul the aged" marched through that Forum in which the voice of Cicero had once rung in prevailing power, he marched not like Cicero when he met his crushing sorrows,—broken down, miserable, and despairing,—but with the step of a conqueror, with the dignity of a king on his coronation morning.

Between the two there was a world-wide difference,—the one man all his life had been resting upon the praise of the creature; the other, all his later life at least, upon the love of the Creator: the one had sought his own glory; the other had sought "the glory of God." Of course the opportunities of the two were very different; Cicero was "nature," Paul was "grace." But what was scarcely blameworthy in Cicero would not be blameless in you. You can act in your measure like Paul, for the same strength is yours. It *has* been done, and what has been done may be done again. I ask, then, the question, Is it your motive? Is it so in any sense? You may say, "It is a high motive;" and therefore I hardly like to answer, "Yes." Stop! Do you get a glimpse of it? Has it in *any* measure come home to you, that motive? Has it ever been your desire, your dream to act more and more for the glory of God? If so, has there then come the thought, "Ah, if I did," what then? External failure? O my brother, blessed failure! Blessed, if ye

> "'Do not blame' the Power
> . . . . . . Which has set this bar
> Betwixt success and failure, for I know
> How far high failure overleaps the bound
> Of low successes.
> Not only those
> Who hold clear echoes of the voice Divine
> Are honourable—they are blest, indeed,
> Whate'er the world has held—but those who hear
> Some fair faint echoes, though the crowd be deaf,
> And see the white god's garments on the hills,
> Which the crowd sees not, though they may not find
> Fit music for their visions; they are blest,
> Not pitiable."

Blessed, if you have caught a vision of God; blessed, if *that* light has come to you. Obey it; let all things collapse, your life be a failure, your reputation gone, only be true to the vision flashed upon you, and believe me you have a motive that will impel you onward steadily and bravely to the end. Better to fail, as men call failure, than to win under God's anathema. Better to live to the high motive, sneered at or despised by man, than to act to a low motive, that may bring you a passing success in the praise of the creature, but make you forget your contribution to the glory of the living God. Too high the motive? Yes, for mortals, but we are immortals, and for immortals it is not too high. Oh, like Paul the aged, be "obedient to the heavenly vision;" do all to "the glory of God."

One further question: "How is such motive strengthened?" My answer is direct. By the faithful suppression of lower substitutes. By forming intentions, by reference to the one worthy standard of a Christian's duty. And therefore by intercourse, persistent, truthful, loving intercourse with God.

My friends, to-day I close these words on the motives of the Christian life, and I cannot forget the season as I close. Christ is coming. Yes, but Christ *has* come. Throw back your mind to the first coming, for already almost are ringing in our ears the chimes of Christmas bells; they come, in echoing *carillon* of change, across the ages of the Church's history, and they remind us of that dear, that ever-fresh and strengthening fact, of the Baby Boy of Bethlehem. Go back in imagination, see the world then. It has two great scenes on which the eye fixes: Rome, with its imperial greatness, with its high ambitions, with its external splendour, then with its gradual, unarrested fall; Bethlehem, with its grey, quiet hills, its silent, lonely cave, the manger, the oxen, and the sleeping Babe on a maiden mother's knee. Which was the greatest? One is gone, collapsed and ruined; the other is triumphant in this church to-day: one was a merely human power; the other was the exaltation of "the glory of God."

Oh, by the Christ, as He came for God's glory, you learn the moral characteristic that will tone your being, if you surrender to the guidance of the motive of the Nativity; and you learn the everlasting benefit given you in return. (1) The moral characteristic is simplicity of character, directness of aim, honesty of purpose, and therefore, a power and an energy of work, which may be the possession of the creature if he lives for the glory of his Creator. (2) And the consequence is not portrayed for us merely, but given to us, at Bethlehem. To work for the glory of God takes us away from the fears, and anxieties, and the perils, that come thick around this mortal life. Other things may be stripped off and torn from you, but one contribution to your life and character will be yours, if you act with this pure motive, that contribution, that priceless benefit is *peace*—peace that "passes understanding;" peace looking calmly on God; peace coming to a heart set to do one thing only, leaving everything else to perish, be it what it may, that God may be glorified. The Christmas bells will soon be rung, but years and centuries ago there came from heaven a sweeter sound than Christmas bells, a sound from out the harmonies of heaven, the music, the chanting of the choir of God. What was it they sang? What was their proclamation? "Glory to God in the highest, peace on earth, good will to men."

And now gather up all that we have thought of. The real *power* of Christian life is grace; the *permanent form* of grace is motive, that implies a vision—the vision of another world; therefore man, for God's sake, loved and lived for; therefore Christ—God in the lineaments of humanity—delighted in, remembered always; therefore God in all things glorified. And further, those acts, and those alone, are of permanent and real value, that have within them the element of Eternity. *That* is of lasting force, which has within it *the* crowning thought, "the glory of God."

Difficult? yes. Mixed motives? yes. The whole thing is supernatural *and* therefore possible. Man is great and little—a complex being. If he act as he may in his highest, his eternal character, his life *must be* his religion, his religion *must be* his life.

And finally, in closing, certain practical reflections remain. If I dared to say that a powerful motive was needed more by one being than another, I would warn you that it is especially necessary to a pliable character. Some are especially endowed with the gift of sympathy, and therefore especially feel its need themselves. They cannot bear to live unloved. This is more or less true of all, in youth. It has its great blessings, *and* its peculiar dangers. Blessings, because it enables men to realize and allow for others' trials; dangers, for it induces them to place too much stress on their approval. One strong motive corrects it, the duty of glorifying God.

The resources at our service are sufficient, but the time of our trial is short. We cannot afford to squander the one or misuse the other. As the years of our mortal pilgrimage are counted up, we must keep one thought before us, "How may I please God?" Ah! we are but poor creatures at the best. But the poorer we, the more is He glorified by our change, our advance, our perfection. He will help us; He changes not, Who is the Source of even our faintest achievement, and the Crown of our final victory.

"Therefore to whom turn we but to Thee, the ineffable Name?
Builder and Maker, Thou, of houses not made with hands!
What, have fear of change from Thee Who art ever the same?
Doubt that Thy power can fill the heart that Thy power expands?
There shall never be one lost good! what was, shall live as before;
The evil is null, is nought, is silence implying sound;
What was good, shall be good, with, for evil, so much good more:
On the earth, the broken arcs; in the heaven, a perfect round."

This we must start with. This we must repeatedly recognise. Whatever be the area, whatever the details of our probation, we have each *one* Master, we are the *servants of God*.

To recognise this as a practical reality, we have two simple guide-posts — the one is the necessity of diligence in *duty*, whatever place we occupy; the other is unflagging, indefatigable activity in the practice of prayer. We are not our own; we are stewards put in trust for a time, to spend all we have for the advantage of another—affections, desires, longings to be lavished on our Creator; opportunities, health, money, abilities to be expended for His honour. To keep the thought of *His* approval before us as a thought of final and sufficient reference, and to do right because it *is* right, is a simple method of doing " all for the glory of God."

How largely, how richly we are endowed may well fill us with apprehension. If the waste be great, the punishment must be proportionate; *and* if there be faithfulness, proportionate the reward. There have been thousands of the miserable, who have had small opportunities; ours, let us remember, are almost excessive.

It is a fearful, but it may be a blessed, thing to be a thriving merchant, or a well-intentioned Christian; for I repeat, the wealth of endowment, in outer or in inward gifts, is the measure of responsibility; the faithful use of possession is the measure of reward. I ask again, what shall guide us, what relieve us in such a terrible position? Only one principle, a simple reference to one object, the prayer, the endeavour to act and live "for the glory of God."

To purify motive may be said to be the work of life.

Certainly the springs of human action are of the most complex, of the most subtle, conceivable. At the best we have reason to fear; our highest motives are far from simple and pure. But a true life, one tending onwards towards ultimate perfection, must take into its reckoning in *all* matters—at least in intention and effect—religious truth. Do not think it beneath your notice to take yourself to task, at fitting times, as to your truth and consistency; that is, " Watch and pray," *not* to be a dexterous manœuverer, " trimming your sails to every breeze," but to be, amid whatever error, a high-principled man. Religion is not merely in devotional exercise, much less in the fatal habit of readiness of tongue in religious phrase. You cannot be self-seeking, worldly, avaricious; you cannot be of an easy morality in matters of daily duty, of lax indifference as to the claims of revealed truth, *and* at the same moment a religious man. Watch your motives; pray and strive for their purity. Ask, in penitence, forgiveness for their weakness or their imperfection. There is no more fatal shipwreck than that to which a life is speeding on which in the midst of religious observance, or with profusion of religious phrases, is careless of the moral claims of duty in the detail of daily acts.

Character, my brothers, is being hourly formed. By our Creator we were made, to express His will we must live. The perfection of the creature is "the glory of God."

By the grace of God, and by that alone—sought and used—can this be obtained. To pray for a deepening sense of responsibility, and a serious conviction of personal weakness, and therefore to make a more constant reference to the source of truth, and to learn more complete dependence upon Him,—is the best way to strengthen and purify the motives of a life.

Therefore, O Lord, help us, for we are helpless; lighten us, for we are in darkness; guide us, for we are frail and erring. Our only hope, our only confidence, we place, O Lord, in Thee.

Dedication.

THIS SERMON IS DEDICATED

TO THE WORKING MEN OF MANCHESTER,

BY ONE

WHO IS THANKFUL TO LABOUR IN ANY, THE SLIGHTEST,

MEASURE FOR THEIR ETERNAL INTERESTS;

AND WHO DESIRES

NO HIGHER CALLING THAN EMPLOYMENT IN THE SERVICE

OF THE GREAT MASTER

AS A WORKING MAN.

St. Alban's Rectory,
October 3, 1877.

SERMON X.[1]

The Claims of Christ.

"Come unto Me, all ye that labour and are heavy laden, and I will give you rest. Take My yoke upon you, and learn of Me; for I am meek and lowly in heart: and ye shall find rest unto your souls."—
ST. MATTHEW xi. 28, 29.

THESE words, my brothers, have come to us across the ages, filled with a power of thrilling tenderness which has carried them to the heart of thousands upon thousands of our fellow-creatures. Whenever any Christian has read them, he has felt instinctively that they conveyed a message with a wider range, a further scope, than the circumstances of their utterance could supply. When our Blessed Redeemer uttered them, He did so first probably to a mixed multitude in Galilee, or to attendant crowds near Nain, or to longing sinners by the lake-side at Magdala—to the same men, it may have been, who had listened to Him denouncing woe against the sin-laden cities (vers. 20-24), who had heard His proclamation of His Father's love manifested in His own Divine person (ver. 27). The time, the place, the

[1] This sermon was preached in Manchester Cathedral, at a special service for the working classes, October 2, 1877.

recipients of His message of compassion may be veiled in uncertainty; but this, at least, is certain, that our Blessed Lord, to whomsoever He spoke *directly* in the first instance, spoke *through* them to all the ages and to all mankind. The men on the lake-side of Galilee—if there indeed it was—to whom this message was primarily addressed, were, then, strictly *representative* men—representative because each one of the assembly had about him, most certainly, some single characteristic feature that belongs to fallen man as man; and it is clear that here our dear Lord's eye pierced beyond the mere immediate range of any special crowd before Him, that His thought was stretched along the intervening years, to individual after individual, endowed with a common humanity, like those to whom He spoke. His message is, in short, a *universal* message; it demands one condition to ensure its appropriate application, and if, in any human being, such condition be fulfilled, then His words are addressed to that man.

Now that one condition, which guarantees the suitability of our Lord's saying to any individual case, is plainly stated in the text, "labouring and heavy laden." If there be one that comes under that description, then to that man, be he saint or be he sinner—to that man to-night, in Manchester, as truly as that day in Galilee, Jesus sends a clear proclamation, Jesus insists upon a mysterious claim.

The proclamation is, "Come unto Me." The question

follows, What is the claim? But before I attempt an answer, let us pause for a moment on some preliminary thoughts.

My friends, to-night, as certain labouring men have asked me, through the proper authority in this church, to speak to them for God, I feel that in addressing those who belong to what are called "the working classes," I preach to men who stand in a kind of symbolic position. For the phraseology of the text means literally "toiling," or "tired with toiling," and "loaded" like a beast of burden, or a freighted ship. Now all men, in one sense or another, are labouring—wearied with work, and sinking under their burdens. All come thus accurately within range of the text: engaged in labour, against sin and for God, or against God and in the pay of sin. Yes, we all are working and weary in this weary and working world. Those, therefore, by common consent designated "the working classes" may be said to hold a strictly symbolic position. They, if any, are *representative* men.

Well, my friends, first of all it may possibly be expected of me, that I should speak to you to-night upon some special topic that touches labour. Perhaps I owe you an apology because I cannot do so. You may wish me, perhaps, to take some account of the "burning questions" of the day—to enter upon those subjects that lie within the wide field of political economy, and bear upon the relation of class to class. Perhaps you will have supposed that it is my duty here to say something upon the artificial methods of raising the market price of labour—something about the difficulties that accrue to one class or the other, in presence of those startling phenomena which have attained such tremendous dimensions in our time, the "strikes" (as we call them) that arise from the quarrels between masters and men. Perhaps you may expect me to speak to you about some of the causes of the commercial depression which affects so many in these days. I can do nothing of the sort. It is impossible for me to say one word of these things, simply for this reason, that, though I am very far indeed from being an uninterested spectator, I am, upon the difficulties and mysteries of such questions, profoundly ignorant. On these subjects *you* can teach *me*, and I shall be proud and thankful to learn; *I* am utterly incapable of teaching *you*. They are deeply interesting, vastly mysterious, big with results in themselves often terribly heartrending. To discuss them ably is undoubtedly important, and indeed indispensable, in the times in which we live, but it is not within my province, or in my power, to do it; I am *not* a political economist, and therefore I cannot deal with them. I *am* a minister of Jesus, and therefore I can speak for Christ.

Well, that being the case, I choose to-night—and I think I choose not wrongly—to put before you these truths: First of all, that a clear *call* comes from Jesus to the working classes of England; and secondly, that a powerful *claim* upon their allegiance is advanced by our Blessed Lord.

Now first, for a moment, as to *the call*. Let us face facts. Thank God, if you and I face facts, in nine cases out of ten we have to be thankful. To look the facts of life in the face earnestly, solemnly, religiously, is, I maintain, in the end to thank God. We have much, doubtless, for which to blame ourselves, many sorrows of our own making; but even sorrows, to the religious mind, become channels of blessing—even in them we have much for which to thank God. And I, when I look the present facts in the face to-night, am filled with thankfulness. It is an evident fact that a call has gone out to the working class of England, from England's ancient and glorious Church. It is a remarkable fact that a change has passed over the spirit of the nation's dream.

There was a time when it was not so. Only a few months ago a French gentleman observed to me, that wherever there is material progress, wherever there is commercial enterprise, there follows a failure in faith, that, as the industries come in, Religion goes out.

I think the statement exaggerated; but there was some truth in it, probably, as regards the great towns of Belgium, and the manufacturing towns of Northern France. I saw it, alas! with my own eyes, in one instance at least. But I am thankful to remember that there is, in the present day, considerably less truth in the statement, even amidst all our sins and sorrows, in the great towns of England. The time was it was not so. In the closing years of the last century, and amidst the religious stagnation of the Hanoverian period, as well as in more recent times, our working classes, and most of our poorer people, were utterly *out* of the Church. Respectable gentlemen closed their pews and locked the doors; and a dead, dull, selfish service had extruded English people from the worship of the English Church. But the days have changed. The Spirit of God has breathed upon the dry bones; the deep below has heard the sound and felt the force of the wind that breathes from the land of God. There has been *a movement*, and *a stir*, and *a rising;* and when I look at the fact that English working men have interested themselves once more in the faith and the fortunes of England's Church, I first of all turn my face in thankfulness to the God Who has done it; for I know that if they are moved out of their lower thoughts, out of their narrow grooves, out of their selfish aims, if they have risen up to desires that are higher, and better, and nobler, and greater, then it is because the voice of Jesus has rung through the ages, and spoken to the hearts of His people, "Come unto Me."

My brothers, first facing that fact, I thank God for what I see to-night.

And then I ask you to go beyond the mere truth of

the call that has been listened to, and attend for a moment to *the claim*. What is the claim of Jesus, my Master, on the working men of England? It is a wide question; it demands a careful answer. My brothers, I cannot answer that question in all the fulness of detail that I would do, if I could, to-night; but there are one or two points that come out before my mind which I suggest to you as a fair answer, so far as they go.

I. The claim of our dear Lord and Master, then, first of all is this—a claim to speak, with authority, The Truth; it is *a dogmatic claim*. Jesus claims to-day, as Jesus claimed in Galilee, not to utter speculative opinion, not to suggest probable presumptions, not to teach anything merely relative, but to speak *dogmatic fact*, to assert revelations of God to which man's intellect and mind should bow, and for which, by their very nature, they crave. "Learn of Me." And when I say *dogmatic facts*, I do not, of course, mean to assert that a dogmatic *system* was *drawn out* by our Blessed Lord during His life. Certainly not. He taught much in person, but He promised that His Spirit would teach more. Men learned as men could bear to learn. The scattered facts revealed by Jesus were harmonized together, and explained in the fulness of their ultimate consequences, by the Holy Spirit, teaching the minds of His commissioned followers. Whether working in person, or by His Spirit, still He is the Revealer, and as such meets the *needs* of man.

Man has a conscience which is given him as a guide *in conduct*, but has no power to *reveal* the Truth. He yearns after, he needs to know, those Majestic Revelations which touch his Creator's nature and his own destiny; truths which are fruitful in moral influence, if he truly grasps them, truths which are instrumental for his sanctification, if he really gazes upon them—truths *towards* which Reason may lead, but *into* which she may not enter; which far transcend, but, by their very superiority, cannot contradict her; which simply, when once they have been received, admit of nothing but entire obedience.

My brothers, the sole duty of the thinking creature to dogmatic fact—when once the authority on which that fact rests has sufficiently manifested its truth and power—is submission of the intellect first, followed, as it will be, by the loving acquiescence of living faith. Argument in such a case is clearly out of place as to the *character* of dogmatic truth. You have a right to argue about many things: it may be your duty to dispute about much; you may doubtless discuss the difficulties, moral, social, political, that present themselves to your minds in the midst of a world so wonderful, and a society so complex, and in a country so advanced and so advancing, as ours; but though argument is right in dealing with difficulties of this sort, before the claims of a properly accredited dogmatic authority, like Jesus Christ, our duty is not to debate but to obey. I submit to you that such is the foremost claim of our Divine Master. He puts Himself forward as able to teach *the* Truth with unerring certainty; to tell man, as man, what man needs to know; to demand therefore from man, as man, an entire submission to, and a loving acquiescence in, all the Revelations which He has made. "Come unto Me, labouring and heavy laden; learn of Me."

And mark, too, how *personal* is the claim. If He teaches you dogmatic truth, He makes Himself the very centre of it all. He is the living embodiment of the truth of God; He is the goal of man's aspirations; He is the ultimate limit of man's attainments. This is so evidently *the* special character of Christianity, that it is needless to dwell upon it; its truths may, indeed, be presented as a system of doctrine, but that dogmatic system is, after all, merely the explanation and expression of a person and a life. The first point, then, in this proclamation of our Divine Redeemer is the claim authoritatively to teach the Truth.

I need scarcely, I suppose, in speaking to Christians, reiterate the fundamental certainty, that the right of Jesus to make any claim at all on mankind has been finally certified by His Resurrection from the dead. We know that *that* is a fact of history, which—not to be theorists, but serious persons—we are bound to respect. We know that it rests upon the testimony of sober-minded, unimaginative, "working men;" and that the effect of it upon themselves was such, as nothing short of such a miracle could have produced. We know that no dexterity of unbelieving criticism has succeeded in invalidating this central fact; and we know it is an unimpeachable certificate of the place and power of the Divine Redeemer, and therefore of His right to advance His claim. The claim, then,—of whatever character and substance be the revelation,—is an imperious claim.

My brethren of the working classes, you value education, you are daily learning to value it more and more. You are not callous to the claims of useful knowledge; you hail with satisfaction the enlargement of modern public feeling on the difficult question of amusements for yourselves, after your weary days and toilsome nights. Well and good. You enter into questions of national interest. You have had in England's history a strange and eventful political education. Good also: thank God for it. You have learned independence of thought, in the severe school in which you have been trained in your great country; and you may begin to fancy yourselves capable of dealing with *any* subject, of solving *any* problems, however intricate; if so, remember there are regions of mystery, regions of beauty and glory, regions of peace and blessedness, on which no reasoning, no argument, no " useful knowledge," as it is called, can of themselves throw any light whatever. You need not discuss them, for you have not the mental capacity; the most learned man who ever lived, unaided by special grace, is unequal to the task.

If it be true that Jesus came and lived, and taught, and toiled, and died, and rose triumphant from the grave; if it be true that He put before you that great central truth of Christianity—namely, that He Himself, Almighty God, came in the flesh and lived and suffered for you because He loved you; and that from that human life of His there flows the power of His Church, the strength of His Sacraments, the meaning of His blessed Word, in fact all the revelation of the Faith—then it is your duty—as earnest, intelligent, active men, God's creatures, understanding how to live and work in this world—to bow down, *bow down*, before the revelation of Jesus. It may be that, having had no teaching, you must ask yourselves first, "What is the Truth that my Lord has revealed?" and if patiently seeking, earnestly desiring, prayerfully striving, longing, looking up for, that truth, then, when it *does* reach you in the authoritative teaching of the Divine Redeemer, it is your duty to bow before it with complete submission, and to accept it and grasp it with a loving faith. It may sound paradoxical, but it is simple fact to say, that the human intellect finds full scope for its activity, and finds also the completeness of rest, only in the Truth. "Come unto Me, all ye that labour and are heavy laden, and I will give you *rest.* Take My yoke upon you, and learn of Me."

Now the claim of Jesus to teach authoritatively has been handed on by His Church. The Church of Jesus at this moment,—divided as it is in the world with a rent here and a trouble there, with darkness, sorrow, controversy, misunderstanding, — yet all the same, with one loud voice, with one steady utterance, proclaims the truth of the Incarnate Redeemer, and witnesses to the great main facts which He has revealed for the guidance of His people. The Church of Jesus, therefore, calls her children in this age to "come" and "learn." It tells them the force of creeds, the value of catechisms; witnesses to them that the exhortation at the time of holy baptism,—used when they first became "members of Christ" by that sacrament,—stating clearly the duty of learning "all other things that a Christian ought to know and believe to his soul's health," is only the Church's way of advancing the unchanging claim of her Divine Master—"Learn of Me."

"Learn of Me." There are tracts of truth that no man can survey, mines of mystery into whose depths no eye can penetrate, regions of wonder that no heart can dream of. Jesus *reveals* them to you; and oh, in your labouring life, oh, in your struggling toil, oh, in your weary days, oh, in your wakeful nights, what it is to have a treasure of unchanging, eternal truth— facts upon which practical men can stand firmly, as upon a rock that will not give way; facts that are witnessed to by the Church of the ages, as sanctioned by the voice of the incarnate God! Jesus proclaims

Himself as a Teacher of truth with authority; that is the first department of His claim.

My brothers, have you ever thought about this claim? has it ever struck you to inquire? Are there any in this church to whom the idea has never presented itself to ask what the meaning of the Church's Faith may be—on what it rests—why it is put forward—*why* a man should be a Churchman, as we call it, at all? Have you ever examined the question? If you *have*,—carefully, patiently, thoughtfully, prayerfully, using such light as you could command,—then, should you dissent from the teaching of the Church, I have no fault to find; I can only pray that God will bring you yet to see the beauty and the glory of the fulness of His Truth. But if you have not, oh, then I say this, "peace in believing" comes to him who grasps with a living faith the Truth, not from speculation, but from a grasp, a loving, faithful grasp of the great facts and consequences of the life of the Incarnate. Other things—political economy, national interests, religious controversies, social fashions, startling events—are mere trifles of the day; they come, they go, they change, they die;—one piece of news this morning, a new paragraph in the paper to-morrow, a nine days' wonder at the most, or a few months of solicitude and anxiety, and then it is gone. But the Faith of the ages, "the Truth as it is in Jesus," the Incarnate Life with all its consequences, oh, that changes not. Oh, *that* as it was powerful in Galilee so it is powerful tonight.

My brother, if you don't know it; if you have never known it; if you have not cared to think about it; if you have fancied it beneath your notice; if you have imagined it was for weaklings, or for women, or for the clergy, or for idle persons, or for highly respectable people who had plenty of time and little to do;—turn your mind to the grandest thought, the greatest subject, with which the world of ideas has ever been enriched—"the Truth as it is in Jesus." "Learn of Me." Such, I repeat, is the first claim of my Master.

II. I pass to the second. You may say to me, if you be a thoughtful man, "You claim for Jesus, the Incarnate, first of all, to have spoken unvarying truth with His own lips, or by His Spirit, and then to have bequeathed it to His Church, to witness to the same for ever. You claim that the Church of England bears her witness truly to that unchanging body of fact revealed by her Divine Lord; that, with whatever weakness, with whatever faultiness, this may be done, yet on the whole the great panorama of Divine Revelation is unfolded by your Church before your eyes?" Yes, my brother, I do.

But now, you may ask me, "Well, if there be any reality in what you say, how am I to grasp and make this truth my own?" Right; it is a fair question.

The answer has been, however, already implied. No

use in accepting the dogma, no use in submitting to the Truth with the intellect alone. We *do* what we *are*, certainly; but it is conversely true that we *are* according as we *do*. As you *act*, so you are sure to *be*. If you accept a truth, that truth has no vitality, no power, no consequence upon your life, till you love it, think it out, *do* it, and so make it tell upon the world.

Then comes the question, How are you to find the strength for such an achievement?

Well, the second claim of the Lord Jesus is a claim that answers the query, a claim that supplements the teaching of the Truth. He claims to be the very centre, the very home of that mysterious power by which truth is grasped, of that mighty influence by which truth is lived. What is that? That is *grace*, the mystery of grace. Jesus claims that we must "come" to Him, because we need the grace of God. Let me urge upon you, how imperative it is that you should face this fact. I know no danger of the time we live in, that compares to the danger of undervaluing the need and energy of grace. I know nothing so startling, so awful in this day of materialistic thought, of what is called "practical effort," than that tremendous peril, lest thoughtful men and women should forget the meaning, the value, the necessity of the grace of God.

Now, what is grace? Grace, some ancient misbelievers asserted, was exterior influence, God's authority, or God's favour and benefit. Grace, modern people reiterate, is something of the same kind; a mere expression for a smile of kindliness, so to speak, on the face of the Creator. Grace is nothing of the sort. Grace is *a power*, an interior power, an internal force; it comes from the life of God; it pierces to the soul of man. It cannot be seen, but it can be felt in its consequences, and verified in its results; and for that reason it is parallel to the forces of nature, with which all are more or less conversant. To borrow an obvious illustration, by no means original: Is any one here tonight who is in the habit of working in the telegraph office? If so, he guides, almost governs, forces which he cannot see; forces he cannot measure, except in their consequences; forces awful and real though unseen; forces the mystery of which he cannot fully explain, although he may register their effects; and so, at his slightest motion of that little needle,—lo! a message is flying across the world! because an influence from the powers of nature is brought to bear on a special object, through the scientific research, and successful efforts of human minds, and under the guidance of a free and energetic will.

Now this is like grace. Grace is a power from the love of God. He "charges" His Church with it—if I may use the simile—in order that the battery of that Church may play upon the soul. Grace is no magical influence; it requires, as it forms, a moral conformity. Grace is no superstitious imagination. Grace is no mere *influence* at all. It is an interior *force*. It is that "well of water springing up unto everlasting life." O my brothers, it is the life, the essential life-force of the great Creator, as it is applied, through the human life of the Incarnate Jesus, giving strength to the sacraments, meaning to the teaching of the Word, force to our prayers, vitality and energy to the poor soul that must stand face to face with its God, and wants the strength to love and act upon His Truth. That is grace.

Now Jesus claims to be the Giver of Grace; and therefore that you should "come" to Him, because you are "labouring and heavy laden," and because you are in need of help.

Let me pause for a moment upon this thought. Divine Grace! Do you know your weakness, my brother, you, working man? You get up in the morning and go to the workshop; you meet your fellows; you have your cup of coffee, or what it may be, on the way, and then you get to work. As to your work, since it is often monotonous and wearisome, you want strength for *duty*. As to your conversation, is it always refined, or at least pure and good? Does it never betoken indifference to a Sacred Presence by its lightness or its blasphemy? Something within you says that *that* blasphemy, which you speak or which you hear, is wrong. Something within you says those evil, filthy words are unworthy of a man, not to say a Christian. You would that you dare witness against them, but you are a coward. What are you to do? Is the Church to denounce you? Is the Church to call you hard names? Is the parson in the pulpit to find fault with you, because you do not perform that difficult task of witnessing to Jesus? I trow not. What do you want? Grace; God's Grace. You can seek it, it will come. Perhaps it makes old memories of God's love revive; it brings back, perhaps, strong feelings of a purer, better past; it tells you, it may be, of another world, of which you dreamed when you were a little child, unspotted by the sin that since has blasted the promise of the years. It flashes through you with a force, an almost electric force, and when you have thrilled responsive to its power, then, my brother, then you are strong. "Come unto Me, all ye that labour and are heavy laden, and I will give you rest." That rest cometh from the grace of God, and it is Jesus Christ Who claims to give it. Such is His further claim.

Another thought on grace. How is it that many men are unable to resist the stern, the relentless, the *desperate* claims of sin? Alas! it is hard to fight the battle of the Christian life. But sin can be resisted, as sin can be forgiven, by that power of grace which takes the Divine objects of contemplation, and marshals them before the mind in so many and such powerful forms. It is possible for you to meet Jesus in the street; possible to find Him in your workshop; possible to have Him as your Friend as you go home; possible for Him to whisper in your ear sacred words of encouragement or of warning; possible for you to receive Him, as an inward gift, to dwell in your hearts. Such is the power of Grace. It takes that intensely fascinating Object—Jesus our Redeemer—and presents Him in one way to one, in another way to another; ever the same, yet ever changing; ever old, yet ever young, fresh and vigorous in His power of battle; so that the Christian, brought into union with that Divine Redeemer, is indeed, as the apostle says, a "new creation," able, in the strength of extended capacities, to cope with the difficulties of life.

Have you asked for God's grace? Have you sought it in His sacraments? Have you petitioned for it in prayer? Have you united in worship in church that you may have it? "Ask, and ye shall receive." You cannot live without Jesus Christ; for the will is weak, and strength is needed; the claim of the Lord is that He *can*, the promise is that He *will*, give, and give in lavish abundance, to the earnest seeker. He is the Teacher of Truth: He is the Giver of Grace. "Come unto Me, all ye that labour and are heavy laden, and I will give you rest."

Now, further, such a fact is fruitful in consequences. If we possess that truth, and drink in that grace, then the position that we are placed in is *a position of dignity*. You want liberty, and Christ is the Emancipator. He lifts you above the trifles of life, and disentangles you from the little things that tie you down to this world.

He helps you so to enter into the sanctuary, that things are changed in meaning, and enhanced in value, to your awakened eyes. Down here in Manchester the mist lies thick, because the smoke spreads its confining canopy above the town. Up there, upon the hills of Yorkshire, you rise above the mist and smoke of cities, see the bright sky, and breathe the pure air of heaven.

So with the soul in grace. Out in the world the working man with his hard black hands and grimy face, must use his strength of arm, or brain, to fight for his bread, to earn his wage, to support his family; but also he is a Christian—he has therefore further work to do; he is bound to rebuke sin; he is pledged to play the man, and no longer act the coward or the slave. He is jeered at by one fellow-workman, because he ventures to rebuke his blasphemy, or protest against foul words unfit for Christian lips; he is laughed at by another, because he revolts against the prevailing pastime of drinking himself drunk, and prefers to seek amusements more fitted for a creature formed on a sacred model, endowed with princely gifts. He, weary, disappointed, dismayed, retires within the sanctuary of the soul. There, he feels that such trifles sit lightly upon him. Troubles come, but they pass away; sorrows settle down like a thick and blinding fog, but the sunlight of God pierces through. He is walking with the step of a conqueror; he is gazing with the eyes of a saint; an illumination of unearthly brilliance is within him.

What is the meaning of this spectacle? What the interpretation of such a phenomenon? It *is* a fact. I have seen it in the cottage of the poor; I have seen it in the mansion of the rich; I have seen it amongst the utterly uneducated; I have seen it in those whose minds are enriched with varied and systematic culture. I have met with it many a time. What is this confronting me? A phenomenon as startling as beautiful: *a real Christian.* Why so earnest? Why so true? Why so fearless? Why so unworldly? Why, with so many things within his reach, will he not stretch his hand to snatch them? Why, so much already grasped, and he flings it all away? Why, the possibility of comfort, and yet the choice of self-sacrifice? What is the meaning of it all? Why not swim with the stream? Why not re-echo the cry of the crowd? Why not join with his companions? Why not drink himself drunk, or curse himself callous, and swear, to lend emphasis, or joke profanely, to win applause? Why not lead a life of impurity, or adopt principles opposed to truth? Why not? I say, Why not?

Ask the question with unflinching persistence, Whence comes that strength? whence that energy? whence that force of character? whence that stalwart virtue? whence that unearthly beauty?

O my brother working man, when I meet you fighting for Jesus; when I see you bearing witness in the world; when I hear that you read your Bible in the morning, and go to your church on Sunday, and prepare for your confirmation, and make ready to "take the Sacrament," as you say, in sweet and homely phrase; when I find you trying to live the life of a good father, of a loving brother, of a faithful husband, of an unfailing friend; when I see you an honest worker, a trustworthy servant, not a professor, or time-server, for unworthy ends; when it is evident that you are sincere, and simple, and true, I say, "Where did that man come from, in the midst of a world like this?" And the answer is clear; his power is drawn from that heart of tenderness, Whose throbs I feel vibrating through the revelation of the text; the face of my Master flashes out upon me, from the face of this my brother. This man has been sitting at the feet of Jesus; he has learned unwavering loyalty from the King of souls; he has drunk at the fountain that ever floweth; *the grace of God* has triumphed in a poor, frail mortal; and because it has triumphed, I see that matchless spectacle—a fearless, earnest, faithful, self-denying, supernatural Christian life.

Scientific men demand, and justly, *verification* of theories. The "theory" of supernatural help from Jesus may be tried by a handy test. The power to conquer evil is a proof charge. He claims to give you grace; the peace and beauty of the Christian spirit *verifies* the Saviour's claim. "Come unto Me, all ye that labour and are heavy laden, and I will give you rest."

Our Master, then, claims to teach Truth in all the ages, first in His visible presence, and now, invisibly, in

His Church witnessing to "the Truth as it is in Jesus." Jesus claimed first,—by actual contact with His own Divine person (when on earth He comforted the weary, pardoned the sinner, healed the sick), claims now,—by His continual indwelling through the Spirit, in the Church, which is His Body—to give grace. And grace is that force which endows with more than mortal strength, which is the mystery of the presence of Jesus, the fulness of pardon, the sweetness of peace, the power by which we live to God. The claim of Jesus then is dogmatic; His claim is also supernatural.

III. I pass on. There is another claim of my Blessed Master better and dearer than all. He advances a claim upon you, my working brother, which is of that strong personal character that can only come from Him Who was pre-eminently "Son of Man." If Jesus were only God He might indeed make the claims I have mentioned; but He is *God and Man*, so that He goes further still. He asks you to "come to Him" with intimate affection, and in times of sorrow, depression, and darkness, and promises to meet you with the tenderness of the heart of a friend. He claims, in fact, to lavish upon you the wealth of *His personal love*. And if He does so, remember that such action is in strict conformity with His habits, when He lived the life of a man amongst men.

Cast your eye back upon the life of Jesus, and what do you see? You see there that He never flattered those who were around Him; He made no platform speeches; He did not seek the suffrages of His fellow-countrymen, so to speak, "upon the hustings;" He did not tell men whose hearts He desired to win, how much He thought of them, and, as we should say, what "fine fellows" they were; as there was no unmerited and truthless praise, so there was never harsh, censorious blame. Why? Because to His large heart, their well-being was a serious reality. Because, in fact, He *loved* them. Again, in intimate relations, He told them plainly of their sins—He never flattered the friends who enjoyed His closest intimacy; but He made them *feel* His penetrating affection; "See how He loved him," was a testimony to the deep reality of a calm, unostentatious sorrow. He was always tender to the weak; kind to the weary; strong for those who were faint; He had compassion on the wreck of womanhood that they thrust before Him in the temple to condemn: "Neither do I condemn thee. Go, and sin no more." He forgave the miserable coward who denied Him in the hour of His peril; He pitied the arch-traitor who betrayed Him to the disaster of His death; He was courteous and gentle to the women who ministered to Him, and could not forget *their* sorrows in the scorching anguish of His own; He was tender and kind to the little children whom they brought for His benediction; true to the prophetic picture of His greatness, "He folded the lambs in His arms." Dear Jesus! It is the *brute* who can maltreat the helpless; it is the *brave man* who is tender to the weak; and He was ever tender to the feeble or suffering; strong, straightforward, loving, outspoken to men; He opposed untruth wherever He met it; He encountered His death, because He advanced on the path of duty, in the very teeth of the clamour of a crowd; He died a martyr amidst acutest agony, because He would not abate one word of God's eternal claim. As Man, it was a noble life; it is a fruitful and blessed one, as God. For what He *was*, that He *is;* coming to us still with His eternal vigour; coming to us with His sweet condescension; coming to us with His tender heart; telling us in our desperation, He is ready to succour; telling us in our weakness, He is "able to save;" warning us in our weariness, "My brother, my friend, I am faithful to love." Dear Jesus! The heart throbs, the eyes fill with tears, at the thought of Thy Divine compassion. O strong and tender! O tender and true! Alas! we are "weary and heavy laden," we are sunk in sorrow, we are overborne with sin, and Thy voice comes to us like the bright home-lights to the wanderer, like the old church bells to the exile, like a whisper that breathes from eternity, in our dreams of a dear dead friend: "Rest, My son; rest, heavy laden; weary one, come unto Me."

Such is the claim of Jesus.

And now, working men of England, your place is a solemn and responsible one, in the present action of your country. You have won your way, through many difficulties doubtless, to a proud position; you have a real power in England's counsels; you are acquiring a real power in England's Church; you have much to be answerable for, as well as much for which to be thankful. Is Jesus accepted as your Lord and Master? Have you recognised His imperial right? Do your hearts beat back responsive, when I name that dearest Name? Do you feel that you yourselves have had, and, ever needing, long to have for ever, *that* love and *that* tenderness which comes from the Man of men? Are you, in fact, learning a deep penitence, a sincere hatred of sin? If you are, what then? what then? I answer, *this:* Jesus will forgive your sins, purify your hearts, help you on to holiness of life.

And what then? What will *you* do for Jesus? That is the question I would beg you to ask yourselves tonight. He has loved you, does love, seeks you, helps you, O sinner. Have you met Him, submitted to Him, found how precious He is to a soul really longing for pardon, really desiring grace? What then? What will *you* do for Jesus, for example, from this service, because you have praised Him, prayed to Him, and heard of Him? Is it all to be nothing?—only a name? Is my Master to stand in the midst of us, "where two or three are gathered together," with that same pale, beautiful, worn, loving face as ever, those bleeding hands, that tender heart, and are we to go away

THE CLAIMS OF CHRIST

and do nothing for Him? I say to those who have not known Him, "Come" to Him; bend the proud will; surrender the life; give up the sin that checks you; ask for His forgiveness. To those who have sought Him, but with a half-hearted love, I say give Him, at least this —the *spirit of self-sacrifice*.

One of the disgraces of England is—that the working men of England do not sufficiently understand the spirit of self-sacrifice. Not many months ago it happened to me, in the course of duty, to enter the house of a working man. The sight that met my eyes can never leave my memory. Upon a low bed there lay a young boy, apparently in the last stages of a deadly disease. In the middle of the room there stood a little child, a tiny little helpless creature, scarcely clothed, wailing piteously, numbed with cold on a bleak February day. Poor little fellow, he could scarcely have been three years old; now too lonely, hopeless, miserable, to do anything but stand and wail; it was a home of want, and sickness, and pain. The furniture was all gone, excepting that bedstead upon which lay the dying boy. The fires were out; the lower rooms were desolate. I had to call kind friends, to succour the stricken lad who lay there sick, and the suffering and deserted child. Shortly after, before we had all left the house, *in* there staggered the father, reeling drunk, into that house of wretchedness, followed soon by her who was the mother of those children, incapable of understanding one word of what we said! And that man had been, I found, earning good wages; that man had had enough to keep his family well, and to lay by for the future; but he had learned nothing of the duty of thrift,—not to say the spirit of self-sacrifice,—and hence, there had died within him the independence, and the sense of duty, that belongs to a true and a loving soul. The picture of such a house would serve, I fear, for the picture of many a workman's home, in these days of improvidence and selfish drunkenness. Working men, if there are some amongst you, who from their unthrift and selfishness have become deadly cowards, let them learn from Jesus the *spirit of sacrifice* which will make them brave.

O my brothers, learn that invigorating lesson from the Man of men: He might have had comfort, and He took hardness. He might have had reputation, and He accepted scorn. He might have had a palace, and He chose the Cross; and *He* was a working man. He worked in the carpenter's shop; He laboured in the little town; He went out to teach, first by His life, and then by His word; and He died for the truth of God, which He taught; died for the grace of God which He had to give; died for the love He bore to you, that you and I might "come" to Him for pardon and for light; might learn and use that noble spirit—the spirit of the self-sacrifice. From that spirit comes honesty; from it comes purity; from it comes strength.

A nation is great, if her people are self-sacrificing. A city is great, if her men learn to sacrifice themselves for the claims of duty. But duty is a hard and cold thing; duty is a dead, a soulless thing until it is touched with that touch of fiery tenderness—the touch of Jesus, our Redeemer and our Lord. "Come unto Me, all ye that labour and are heavy laden, and I will give you rest."

And further: I said, that speaking to the working classes I could only tell them the old, old story, because I am simply a messenger for Christ. I add this word, a part of the same message. People when they talk of "the working classes" think that they have described the whole thing with one touch. They imagine that, like the "enter such and such a one" in Shakespeare's stage directions, when they have said "the working classes," then everything by way of definition that is to be said, *is* said. They label the article, so to speak, and then expect you to understand all about it. How difficult it is indeed to bridge across the chasm between class and class! But more difficult it is to remember that "the working class," or any class, is made up of individual souls. Our dear Lord did not speak to *classes* only. Jesus spoke to *souls*. He took men one by one, and each finite creature with his infinite future, each immortal being with his own history, his own work, his own sins, his own feelings, his own sorrows, was an object of tender interest to Jesus Christ. It is so to-night. When a man realizes *that*, when he says, " It is

I myself whom Jesus loves and teaches; He speaks to *me;*" when he recollects that he holds a place in God's ever-watchful care, fills a niche in God's temple, exercises a duty by God's appointment, then, oh then, and not before, he is able to rise, able to respond to the call and the claim of tenderness, not only to go to Jesus, but to act conformably to His claim.

Will you remember that He speaks to you *individually;* will you remember that *your* soul is as valuable in God's sight, my brother, as any soul can possibly be; that He loves *you* with deep Divine affection, desires to feed *you* with His sacraments, to teach *you* by His Word that He calls *you* to His Church, begs *you* to witness to His truth by a life of holiness, of self-sacrifice, of purity, resting on His strength, drawn on, and comforted by, His love and tenderness?

And then there is the end. What does He give you more? Grant that you have accepted Him, grant that you have looked up to Him, that you have come to Him with your sins, brought Him your sorrows, asked Him for His grace, pleaded His mercy, learned to love Him for His Divine compassion, realized the meaning of His life and His sacrifice—what will He give you then? Do you want anything beyond that love? Cannot you lose self in the thought of your Redeemer? Well and good; but in that, with that, He gives you more. "Come unto Me, all ye that labour and are heavy laden, and I will give you *rest.*"

My brothers, things given in this world belong to exterior life. The claims of family die away in the darkness of death. Reputation, what is it but a mere bubble, blown and burst in the first breath of popular indignation, after popular favour? Name and fame, what are they at best, but a passing memory in dying minds? Position and place, what can they supply, but a comfort never really satisfying an immortal creature? They are external; they peel off, they pass away.

But that which is internal, that which touches the seat of the life, that which belongs to the man *himself*, that which can be inwoven in the very texture of his soul, does that pass? Oh, no! When the sounds of political discussion have died away in the distance of receding years, when all social questions have sunk into the abysmal darkness of the past, when all domestic troubles have paled and faded in the far, far horizons of fleeting time, there remains a treasure that will never leave the soul which has firmly embraced it, and that blessed treasure is the "peace that passeth understanding," the "rest that remaineth for the people of God." As the world cannot give it, so the world cannot take it; it is the gift of Jesus; it is the eternal possession of the redeemed.

One word more. My brothers, in your working hours you are often weary with your toil; you work all day; the night comes; you lie down to rest. Think for a moment to-night of that old parable of sleep that reminds you how "man goeth forth to his work and to his labour *until* the evening;" yes, *until* the evening, *then* the work is done.

Not so long ago I addressed vast congregations in this Cathedral during the Manchester Mission; and some of those who listened to me then, strong, healthy, apparently able to choose or leave their God, to listen to the call, acknowledge the claim, or refuse it, or deny, have gone to their account. To-night, again, as God enables, I speak for Jesus to the working men. My brothers, your day of life is going on, like your day of labour. Your mind may, perhaps, be filled with the thoughts and struggles of the passing moment. Oh, for one instant, in God's Church, look on to the setting of the sun, and the closing of the day of labour, in the sleep of the grave. What then? What is beyond? Will all your commercial enterprise, will all ' your passionate longings, will all your political enthusiasms, will all your domestic pleasures, will all your sensual satisfactions, will all your cold, selfish aims, *then* support you? Will the mere dreams of great social questions stand by you as realities? Will your pride, your independence, your self-seeking, bear you up? Will the teaching of the daily papers—now so infallible, now of such commanding interest—be by you to keep the mind at rest, as there rise before it the undreamt-of wonders which spread themselves before dying eyes? I do not say that all such things as I have mentioned are unworthy of attention. Far from it. But are they ultimately trustworthy props for a dying man in the moment of dissolution?

That night you will stand alone; but your work will not be gone, it will come up, accumulating upon you, in full meaning and consequence—the moments of temptation, the sudden falls, the horrid acts of selfishness, the base dishonesty, the cruel unkindness, the evil blasphemy, the intemperate indulgence, the sensual sins, the neglect of church, the thoughtlessness of prayer, the disregard of God, the addiction to all that is defiling and degrading, the contempt of all that is ennobling and pure;—these memories will come up and crowd around you then, dark, ghastly, tremendous. Have you realized the fact? Any man who has not tried to realize that supreme moment, O my brother, forgive me, that man, be he who he may, is, to my thinking, a fool. Realize that moment—the coming of the Lord. Then, you will want to grasp truth that can never change; truth, not mere speculation; truth, not passing opinion; truth that cannot be gainsaid or doubted. You will want grace, to fill your soul with the strength so sorely needed for the journey and the judgment.

You will want more; you will yearn for One to stand by you, a kind face to look upon you, a warm hand to grasp you. Oh, that face looks upon you to-night; that hand is stretched out to you to-night. Labouring brother, labouring at work that is harder than any mechanical toil in the workshops of Manchester, labouring in the throes of sin and sorrow, listen to the voice, stretch out the hand, respond to the sovereign claim of Jesus the Redeemer. At least do this. Kneel, and give Him to-night one thought of thankfulness, one thought of sorrow, one thought of desire. "Come unto Me, all ye that labour and are heavy laden," He says, "and I will give you rest."

> "Labouring and heavy laden,
>   Wanting strength in time of need,
> Fainting by the way from hunger,
>   Bread of Life, on Thee we feed.
>
> Thou the grace of life supplying,
>   Thou the strength for life wilt give;
> Dead to self, and daily dying,
>   Life of Life, in Thee we live."

My brother, who are a real Christian, *you* know it; you know that you live in Him; you know what He is to you; then show it in your life. Make your fellow-workers feel it—that Jesus is all in all, in life, in death, in eternity. My brother, who are *not* a real Christian, you do not know it. Oh, go to Him to-night. Give up the sin that hinders; cut off the habit that checks; go and ask Him to help you to grasp the one reality, to work at the one real, tremendous undertaking; "work while it is called 'to-day;' the night is coming when none can work." Kneel and see the face of Jesus; seeing, you will love Him; loving Him, all will be well. Why neglect Him? Why despise Him? He loves you with a love that will never slacken, never grow dim. Answer it back with your heart's best affection; it will dwarf all this world's objects, it will hush the storms of passion, silence the cry of fear; it will find its full, its final expression in the joy and the thanksgiving of the timeless ages, when cleansed, sanctified, glorified, you stand in the presence of God.

"Blessed are the dead that die in the Lord: Yea, saith the Spirit, that they may *rest* from their *labours;* and their works do follow them."

www.ingramcontent.com/pod-product-compliance
Lightning Source LLC
Chambersburg PA
CBHW032212230426
43672CB00011B/2526